Vocabulary
Power Plus
for the New SAT:

Vocabulary, Reading, and Writing Exercises for High Scores

Book Four

By Daniel A. Reed

Edited by Paul Moliken

ISBN 978-1-58049-256-0

Revised March, 2006

PRESTWICK HOUSE, INC.
"Everything for the English Classroom!"

P.O. Box 658 • Clayton, DE 19938
(800) 932-4593 • www.prestwickhouse.com

Table of Contents

INTRODUCTION

*V*ocabulary Power Plus for the New SAT combines classroom-tested vocabulary drills with reading and writing exercises designed to prepare students for the revised Scholastic Assessment Test; however, *Vocabulary Power Plus for the New SAT* is a resource for all students—not just those who are college bound or preparing for the SAT I. This series is intended to increase vocabulary, improve grammar, enhance writing, and boost critical reading skills for students at all levels of learning.

Critical Reading exercises include lengthy passages and detailed questions. We use SAT-style grammar and writing exercises and have placed the vocabulary words in a non-alphabetical sequence.

To reflect the changes to the Writing and Critical Reading portions of the SAT I, Prestwick House includes inferential exercises instead of the analogical reasoning sections. Coupled with words-in-context activities, inferences cultivate comprehensive word discernment by prompting students to create contexts for words instead of simply memorizing definitions.

The writing exercises in *Vocabulary Power Plus for the New SAT* are process-oriented, but they bring students a step closer to SAT success by exposing them to rubrics that simulate those of the SAT essay-writing component. This exposure to an objective scoring process helps students to develop a concrete understanding of writing fundamentals.

We hope that you find the *Vocabulary Power Plus for the New SAT* series to be an effective tool for teaching new words and an exceptional tool for preparing for the new SAT.

Strategies for Completing Activities

Roots, Prefixes, and Suffixes

A knowledge of roots, prefixes, and suffixes can give readers the ability to view unfamiliar words as mere puzzles that require only a few simple steps to solve. For the person interested in the history of words, this knowledge provides the ability to track word origin and evolution. For those who seek to improve vocabulary, this knowledge creates a sure and lifelong method; however, there are two points to remember:

1. Some words have evolved through usage, so present definitions might differ from what you infer through an examination of the roots and prefixes. The word *abstruse*, for example, contains the prefix *ab* (away) and the root *trudere* (to thrust), and literally means *to thrust away*. Today, *abstruse* is used to describe something that is hard to understand.

2. Certain roots do not apply to all words that use the same form. If you know that the root *vin* means "to conquer," then you would be correct in concluding that the word *invincible* means "incapable of being conquered"; however, if you tried to apply the same root meaning to *vindicate* or *vindictive*, you would be incorrect. When analyzing unfamiliar words, check for other possible roots if your inferred meaning does not fit the context.

Despite these considerations, a knowledge of roots and prefixes is one of the best ways to build a powerful vocabulary.

Critical Reading

Reading questions generally fall into several categories.

1. *Identifying the main idea or the author's purpose.* Generally, the question will ask, "What is this selection about?"

In some passages, the author's purpose will be easy to identify because the one or two ideas leap from the text; however, other passages might not be so easily analyzed, especially if they include convoluted sentences. Inverted sentences (subject at the end of the sentence) and elliptical sentences (words missing) will also increase the difficulty of the passages, but all these obstacles can be overcome if readers take one sentence at a time and recast it in their own words. Consider the following sentence:

> These writers either jot down their thoughts bit by bit, in short, ambiguous, and paradoxical sentences, which apparently mean much more than they say—of this kind of writing Schelling's treatises on natural philosophy are a splendid instance; or else they hold forth with a deluge of words and the most intolerable diffusiveness, as though no end of fuss were necessary to make the reader understand the deep meaning of their sentences, whereas it is some quite simple if not actually trivial idea, examples of which may be found in plenty in the popular works of Fichte, and the philosophical manuals of a hundred other miserable dunces.

If we edit out some of the words, the main point of this sentence is obvious.

> These writers either jot down their thoughts bit by bit, in short, sentences, which apparently mean much more than they say or they hold a deluge of words as though necessary to make the reader understand the deep meaning of their sentences

Some sentences need only a few deletions for clarification, but others require major recasting and additions; they must be read carefully and put into the reader's own words.

> Some in their discourse desire rather commendation of wit, in being able to hold all arguments, than of judgment, in discerning what is true; as if it were a praise to know what might be said, and not what should be thought.

After studying it, a reader might recast the sentence as follows:

> In conversation, some people desire praise for their abilities to maintain the conversation rather than their abilities to identify what is true or false, as though it were better to sound good than to know what is truth or fiction.

2. Identifying the stated or implied meaning. *What is the author stating or suggesting?*

The literal meaning of a text does not always correspond with the intended meaning. To understand a passage fully, readers must determine which meaning—if there is more than one—is the intended meaning of the passage. Consider the following sentence:

If his notice was sought, an expression of courtesy and interest gleamed out upon his features; proving that there was light within him and that it was only the outward medium of the intellectual lamp that obstructed the rays in their passage.

Interpreted literally, this Nathaniel Hawthorne metaphor suggests that a light-generating lamp exists inside of the human body. Since this is impossible, the reader must look to the metaphoric meaning of the passage to understand it properly. In the metaphor, Hawthorne refers to the human mind—consciousness—as a lamp that emits light, and other people cannot always see the lamp because the outside "medium"—the human body—sometimes blocks it.

3. Identifying the tone or mood of the selection. *What feeling does the text evoke?*

To answer these types of questions, readers must look closely at individual words and their connotations; for example, the words *stubborn* and *firm* share almost the same definition, but a writer who describes a character as *stubborn* rather than *firm* is probably suggesting something negative about the character.

Writing

The new SAT allocates only twenty-five minutes to the composition of a well-organized, fully developed essay. Writing a satisfactory essay in this limited time requires facility in quickly determining a thesis, organizing ideas, and producing adequate examples to support the ideas.

An essay written in twenty minutes might not represent the best process writing—an SAT essay might lack the perfection and depth that weeks of proofreading and editing give to research papers. Process is undoubtedly important, but students must consider the time constraints of the SAT. Completion of the essay is just as important as organization, development, and language use.

The thesis, the organization of ideas, and the support make the framework of a good essay. Before the actual writing begins, writers must create a mental outline by establishing a thesis, or main idea, and one or more specific supporting ideas (the number of ideas will depend on the length and content of the essay). Supporting ideas should not be overcomplicated; they are simply ideas that justify or explain the thesis. The writer must introduce and explain each supporting idea, and the resultant supporting paragraph should answer the *why?* or *who cares?* questions that the thesis evokes.

Once the thesis and supporting ideas are identified, writers must determine the order in which the ideas will appear in the essay. A good introduction usually explains the thesis and briefly introduces the supporting ideas. Explanation of the supporting ideas should follow, with each idea in its own paragraph. The final paragraph, the conclusion, usually restates the thesis or summarizes the main ideas of the essay.

Adhering to the mental outline when the writing begins will help the writer organize and develop the essay. Using the Organization and Development scoring guides to evaluate practice essays will help to reinforce the process skills. The Word Choice and Sentence Formation scoring guides will help to strengthen language skills—the vital counterpart to essay organization and development.

Pronunciation Guide

a — track
ā — mate
ä — father
â — care
e — pet
ē — be
i — bit
ī — bite
îr — steer
o — job
ō — wrote
ô — port, horse, **fought**
ōō — proof
ŏŏ — book
u — pun
ū — **you**
û — purr
ə — about, system, supper, circus
oi — toy

Word List

Lesson 1
arable
camaraderie
desiccate
equanimity
frangible
interminable
litany
lugubrious
moratorium
replete
truncate
ubiquitous
vernacular
wrenching
zealous

Lesson 2
brigand
carte blanche
contemptuous
cosmopolitan
donnybrook
incantation
interlocutor
metamorphosis
nomenclature
nonchalant
procrustean
rife
sophistry
stygian
vestige

Lesson 3
abstemious
archaic
atelier
axiom
dulcet
expurgate
iniquity
patronizing
pellucid
peremptory
perspicacious
scapegoat
talisman
usurp
vacillate

Lesson 4
apocryphal
catharsis
crepuscular
efficacious
estrange
internecine
intrinsic
inundate
kudos
maxim
putrid
revere
risible
servile
sybaritic

Lesson 5
anomaly
compendium
comprise
consternation
coterie
disconcert
eidetic
expiate
flippancy
foist
incongruous
innocuous
plethora
preamble
vitriolic

Lesson 6
accoutrement
antediluvian
contrive
haughty
hubris
imbroglio
peregrination
platitude
prognosticate
quotidian
sanctimonious
scullion
sectarian
stringent
venerate

Lesson 7
anecdote
churlish
coeval
cogent
convoluted
dilatory
entreat
gibberish
incumbent
inimical
livid
lurid
nexus
promulgate
staid

Lesson 8
aleatory
allay
ameliorate
asperity
exegesis
inveigh
lionize
otiose
pander
profligate
puerile
recalcitrant
renunciation
unimpeachable
vitiate

Lesson 9
benign
blithe
bumpkin
corroborate
culpable
frenetic
hortatory
indecorous
orotund
penultimate
pervasive
provocative
recrimination
soporific
toady

Lesson 10
circuitous
circumlocution
depredate
indolent
largesse
luminous
majordomo
perambulate
perquisite
polemical
probity
tacit
timorous
untenable
veneer

Lesson 11
bulwark
canard
cortege
crescendo
demotic
disingenuous
dogged
etymology
impresario
intransigent
malaise
requisite
simian
solecism
wont

Lesson 12
assiduous
bellicose
compunction
condescending
epiphany
panacea
physiognomy
propensity
pulchritude
revel
rhapsodize
sepulcher
umbrage
voluble
wizened

Lesson 19	Lesson 20	Lesson 21
abjure	acme	abrogate
dissipate	cerebral	analects
extant	conundrum	anomie
fulsome	deleterious	apostasy
inchoate	discerning	cognizant
inveterate	echelon	extrinsic
propitious	hypocrisy	factotum
rescind	idyllic	febrile
schism	malinger	magniloquent
spurious	nondescript	outré
stentorian	punitive	parity
transient	relegate	propinquity
tremulous	serendipity	prosaic
unwieldy	soluble	supine
utilitarian	waive	surreptitious

Lesson One

1. **camaraderie** (kä mə rä´ də rē) *n.* rapport and goodwill
   The coach attributed the team's success to the *camaraderie* among the players.
   syn: friendship; amity   *ant: enmity; hostility*

2. **frangible** (fran´ jə bəl) *adj.* fragile; easy to break
   Mom seldom used the *frangible*, antique dishes in the china cabinet.
   syn: delicate; breakable   *ant: sturdy; strong*

3. **litany** (li´ tə nē) *n.* any long, repetitive, or dull recital
   The dissatisfied customer read a *litany* of complaints to the company representative.

4. **moratorium** (mor ə tōr´ ē əm) *n.* a suspension of activity; an authorized delay
   The warring factions declared a *moratorium* on combat during the peace talks.
   syn: postponement; cessation   *ant: rush; continuation*

5. **zealous** (zel´ əs) *adj.* fervent; fanatical
   The *zealous* gardener planted so many flowers that a number of them did not have the necessary space in which to grow.
   syn: passionate; enthusiastic   *ant: uninterested; indifferent*

6. **desiccate** (des´ i kāt) *v.* to dry out; to remove moisture
   Janet *desiccates* flowers and then uses them to make wreaths.
   syn: dehydrate   *ant: moisten; dampen*

7. **wrenching** (rench´ ing) *adj.* causing mental or physical pain
   The *wrenching* photographs of the starving children prompted Mike to send a donation.
   syn: distressing; agonizing   *ant: pleasant; comforting*

8. **replete** (ri plēt´) *adj.* full; abundant
   The anglers were happy to find their stream *replete* with trout.
   syn: abounding; rife   *ant: lacking; empty*

9. **interminable** (in tûr´ mə nə bəl) *adj.* tiresome and long; seemingly
   endless
   The last few hours of school before the holiday vacation seemed
   interminable.
   syn: tedious   *ant: fleeting; limited*

10. **arable** (ar´ ə bəl) *adj.* suitable for cultivation of land
    Death Valley and the Badlands are both characterized by their lack of
    arable soil.
    syn: fecund; fertile   *ant: barren; infertile*

11. **lugubrious** (lōō gōō´ brē əs) *adj.* mournful; gloomy
    The *lugubrious* funeral scene temporarily interrupted the comic tone of
    the play.
    syn: somber; depressing   *ant: joyful*

12. **truncate** (trung´ kāt) *v.* to shorten
    The candidate *truncated* his campaign because of a family illness.
    syn: abridge; abbreviate   *ant: lengthen; increase*

13. **ubiquitous** (yōō bik´ wi təs) *adj.* occurring or seeming to occur
    everywhere; omnipresent
    The camping trip was horrible; the mosquitoes were *ubiquitous* and
    hungry.
    syn: universal   *ant: nonexistent*

14. **vernacular** (vər nak´ yə lər) *n.* everyday language
    Using slang or *vernacular* in a formal term paper is usually inappropriate.

15. **equanimity** (ēk wə nim´ i tē) *n.* composure; calmness
    Oddly enough, the plaintiff recounted the story of her attack with perfect
    equanimity.
    syn: sangfroid; poise   *ant: anxiety; agitation*

EXERCISE I—Words in Context

From the list below, supply the words needed to complete the paragraph. Some words will not be used.

litany	truncate	lugubrious	camaraderie
equanimity	interminable	zealous	

1. Tony brushed the rain off his jacket as he walked through the glass doors to the school. It was a[n] _____ Saturday morning, so Tony was happy that the assessment test wouldn't cause him to forfeit a beautiful spring day. He sat down with his answer booklet, and the test proctor began the standard, twenty-minute _____ of instructions, as though the _____, four-hour test were not long enough without the elaborate instructions. Tony, not at all nervous after having taken the test three times already, listened to the proctor with _____; however, some of the more _____ test-takers anxiously tapped their #2 pencils, eager to begin filling in the hundreds of tiny circles on their answer sheets.

From the list below, supply the words needed to complete the paragraph. Some words will not be used.

frangible	wrenching	arable	ubiquitous
replete	vernacular	zealous	

2. Abby had taken Spanish in high school, but she had trouble understanding the shopkeeper's _____. The little shop was _____ with the things that tourists often needed, such as film, medicine, and long-distance phone cards; a shelf in front of the counter contained the keychains, coffee mugs, and tee shirts _____ in every souvenir shop. A row of _____ vases and pottery on a shelf behind the counter caught Abby's eye, but she had actually come in to ask about the exotic plants growing in the _____ plot outside, behind the store.

From the list below, supply the words needed to complete the paragraph. Some words will not be used.

litany   truncate   camaraderie   wrenching
moratorium   arable   desiccate

3. The sporadic rain caused a[n] _____ in the stock car race until workers could _____ the concrete track using large blowers pulled by tractors. While the track dried, spectators watched the _____ among members of the pit crews as they scrambled to make frantic adjustments to cars in the minutes before drivers could return to the track. Despite the excitement in the air, the whole scene was depressing for Miles, a former driver who had to watch the race from the stands. The eight titanium pins holding his leg bones together never let him forget the _____ injury that had _____ his once-promising racing career.

EXERCISE II—Sentence Completion

Complete the sentence in a way that shows you understand the meaning of the italicized vocabulary word.

1. When Angie complained about having to do chores for her allowance, her dad began his usual *litany* about…

2. It's difficult to maintain one's *equanimity* when…

3. The cooler at the picnic was *replete* with…

4. Dirk began to question the *camaraderie* of his teammates when one of them…

5. The actor became frustrated when the *ubiquitous* tabloid reporters…

6. Anita wanted a home with an *arable* yard where she could…

7. The *interminable* wait at the checkout line made Raymond decide…

8. When you pack the boxes for the move, put the *frangible* items…

9. Between innings, one of the *zealous* fans at the game…

10. Bill likes comic poems, but Sylvia prefers *lugubrious* ones that…

11. The NCAA imposed a brief *moratorium* on football games when several athletes...

12. Shelly used common *vernacular* to identify the animals, but the zoology professor wanted her to...

13. You will need to *truncate* your award speech if you find out...

14. Giles tried to suppress his *wrenching* memories of...

15. The pioneers *desiccated* some of the fish so that they...

EXERCISE III—Roots, Prefixes, and Suffixes

Study the entries and answer the questions that follow.

The prefix *ortho* means "straight" or "correct."
The prefix *hetero* means "different."
The prefix *homo* means "same."
The roots *dogm* and *dox* mean "belief."
The root *gen* means "type."
The suffix *logy* means "word."

1. *Using literal translations as guidance, define the following words without using a dictionary.*

   A. dogmatic   D. orthodox
   B. heterodox   E. doxology
   C. homogenous   F. heterogeneous

2. If *para* means "beyond," then a *paradox* is something that is
   _____.

3. List as many words as you can think of that begin with the prefix *ortho*.

4. What is *homogenized* milk?

5. Give an example of a *dogma*.

6. List as many words as you can think of that contain the root *gen*.

EXERCISE IV—Inference

Complete the sentences by inferring information about the italicized word from its context.

1. That is a *ubiquitous* species of tree, so don't be surprised if, during your vacation abroad, you...

2. If you have *arable* ground on your property, then you might consider...

3. If you are bored, and the weather is *lugubrious*, you might...

Exercise V—Writing

Here is a writing prompt similar to the one you will find on the writing portion of the SAT:

Plan and write an essay based on the following statement:

> Books are the best type of the influence of the past, and perhaps we shall get at the truth—learn the amount of this influence more conveniently—by considering their value alone.
>
> –Ralph Waldo Emerson:
> "The American Scholar"

Assignment: In an essay, explain whether you agree or disagree with Emerson's suggestion that books are the best type of influence of the past. Include a comparison of books with other methods of gaining knowledge or understanding history, and explain why books do or do not have the value that they did in 1837, the year of Emerson's quote. Support your opinion using evidence from your reading, studies, observations, and experience.

Thesis: Write a one-sentence response to the above assignment. Make certain this sentence offers a clear statement of your position.

Example: Although books are excellent tools for presenting history, continual advancements in practical technology are the best types of influences from the past.

Organizational Plan: If your thesis is the point on which you want to end, where does your essay need to begin? List the points of development that are inevitable in leading your reader from your beginning point to your end point. This is your outline.

Draft: Use your thesis as both your beginning and your end. Following your outline, write a good first draft of your essay. Remember to support all of your points with examples, facts, references to reading, etc.

Review and revise: Exchange essays with a classmate. Using the scoring guide for Organization on page 248, score your partner's essay (while he or she scores yours). Focus on the organizational plan and use of language conventions. If necessary, rewrite your essay to improve the organizational plan and your use of language.

Identifying Sentence Errors

Identify the grammatical error in each of the following sentences. If the sentence contains no error, select answer E.

1. Many individual's believe that if they are polite to their neighbors, they
         (A)   (B)   (C)
   can be impolite to their families.   No error
      (D)   (E)

2. The commonly known expression that "a dog is a man's best friend" is
          (A)   (B)
   frequently incorrect; all a person has to do is read the newspaper.
        (C)   (D)
   No error
   (E)

3. The home run Hal hit flew out of the stadium sailed into the parking lot,
     (A)   (B)   (C)
   and smashed the window of a brand-new car.   No error
                  (D)   (E)

4. Until one of the members of the rival gangs propose a truce, there will be
           (A)   (B)
   no safety for honest citizens of this city.   No error
       (C)   (D)   (E)

5. No matter how hard Theresa tries, she cannot win the approval of her
        (A)   (B)   (C)
   field hockey coach.   No error
     (D)   (E)

Improving Sentences

The underlined portion of each sentence below contains some flaw. Select the answer that best corrects the flaw.

6. <u>Scientists think of the underwater world beneath the sea as a vast laboratory</u>, in which strange creatures do odd, unexplained things.
   A. Scientists believe the underwater world beneath the sea is a vast laboratory
   B. Scientists feel that the underwater world beneath the sea is a vast laboratory
   C. Scientists think the underwater world is a vast laboratory
   D. A vast laboratory is how scientists view the underwater world beneath the sea
   E. Beneath the sea lies a vast laboratory

7. Ben Franklin was a statesman, politician, printer, author, philosopher, inventor, and Ambassador to France, <u>yet most people studying history in school only think of him as a man standing in a lightning storm with a kite and a key.</u>
   A. yet only most people that study history in school think of him as a man standing in a lightning storm with a kite and a key.
   B. yet most people who studies history think of him as a man standing in a lightning storm with a kite and a key.
   C. yet most people with only a tiny knowledge of high school history think of him as a man standing in a lightning storm with a kite and a key.
   D. yet most people who don't know much history only think of him as a man standing in a lightning storm with a kite and a key.
   E. yet most students think of him only as a man standing in a storm with a kite and a key.

8. "The reason I choose not to," said the potential customer to the car sales-man, <u>"is because of the fact that you have not given me enough for my trade-in."</u>
   A. "Is because of the fact that you have not given me enough for my trade-in."
   B. "is because of you having not given me enough for my trade-in."
   C. "is because you have not given me enough for my trade-in."
   D. "is that you have not given me enough for my trade-in."
   E. "is because of the fact that you aren't giving me enough for my trade-in."

9. There is only one prerequisite for the <u>job; You must have a college degree in Physics.</u>
   A. job: you must have a college degree in physics.
   B. job; you must have a college degree in Physics.
   C. job. That is that you must have a college degree in Physics.
   D. job; You must have a college degree in physics.
   E. job, and it is that a college degree in physics is necessary.

10. <u>Ever since he has devoted himself entirely to helping the homeless.</u>
    A. Ever since he has devoted himself entirely to helping the homeless, he has been happy.
    B. Ever since, he has devoted himself entirely to helping the homeless.
    C. He has devoted himself entirely to helping the homeless.
    D. Ever since he has entirely devoted himself to helping the homeless.
    E. Ever since helping the homeless, he has devoted himself entirely to it.

Lesson Two

1. **metamorphosis** (met ə môr´ fə sis) *n.* a transformation or dramatic change
That butterfly will experience a physical *metamorphosis* as it passes from the pupa stage to the adult stage.
syn: mutation   *ant: stasis*

2. **donnybrook** (don´ ē brŏŏk) *n.* a fight; an uproar
During the last minute of the close championship game, a referee's foolish decision caused a *donnybrook* among the fans of both teams.
syn: brawl; quarrel; altercation   *ant: agreement*

3. **nonchalant** (non shə länt´) *adj.* unconcerned; indifferent
The *nonchalant* banker looked at the million-dollar check as though he saw one every day.
syn: detached; relaxed   *ant: excited; concerned; alarmed*

4. **vestige** (ves´ tij) *n.* a trace or evidence of something that once existed
The rich vein of coal is a *vestige* of Earth's lush, prehistoric forests.
syn: remnant; hint

5. **interlocutor** (in tər lok´ yə tər) *n.* someone who participates in a conversation
The delusional man wandered down the street, conversing with some invisible *interlocutor*.

6. **procrustean** (prō krəs´ tē ən) *adj.* strictly disregarding individual differences or circumstances
The *procrustean* teacher warned the class that he would accept no excuses for tardiness.
syn: ruthless; undiscriminating   *ant: sympathetic; compassionate*

7. **stygian** (sti´ jē ən) *adj.* dark and forbidding
The *stygian* house, empty for decades, was often the source of unexplained phenomena.
syn: shadowy   *ant: bright; illuminated*

8. **sophistry** (sä´ fə strē) *n.* a deliberately deceptive or misleading argument
The TV talk-show host's convincing *sophistry* made his guests look foolish for disagreeing with him.
syn: chicanery; ruse   *ant: truth*

9. **carte blanche** (kärt blänch´) *n.* boundless authority; unlimited power to act
The secret agent had *carte blanche* to complete the extremely vital mission.
syn: license; sanction; free rein   *ant: restriction*

10. **incantation** (in kan tā´ shən) *n.* a chant; a recited magical spell
The sorceress uttered a long *incantation* as she mixed the magic potion.
syn: invocation

11. **cosmopolitan** (koz mə pol´ i tn) *adj.* worldly; sophisticated
Brett longed to have the *cosmopolitan* lifestyle of an international investor.
syn: cultured   *ant: provincial*

12. **rife** (rīf) *adj.* abundant; prevalent
Be careful while shopping, because that part of the city is *rife* with crime.
syn: overflowing; rampant   *ant: lacking; limited*

13. **nomenclature** (nō´ mən klā chər) *n.* technical names or naming system in an art or science
Students often spend hours memorizing the *nomenclature* of organic chemistry.
syn: terminology

14. **brigand** (brig´ ənd) *n.* a robber or bandit
The stagecoach driver kept a nervous watch for *brigands* while transporting the heavy cash box.
syn: highwayman; outlaw

15. **contemptuous** (kən temp´ chōō əs) *adj.* haughty; scornful
The *contemptuous* bank loan officer was rude to the poorly dressed applicants.
syn: arrogant; derisive   *ant: humble; polite*

EXERCISE I—Words in Context

From the list below, supply the words needed to complete the paragraph. Some words will not be used.

donnybrook	cosmopolitan	carte blanche	vestige
procrustean	incantation	metamorphosis	

1. Mr. Trunk, the new manager, walked into his new, albeit antiquated, office. The only _____ of the former manager was a dusty hotrod calendar, three years out of date. Recruited for his _____ leadership style and general lack of compassion, Mr. Trunk promised the company president that production would experience a[n] _____ for the better before the end of the year. Trunk had _____ to change operations any way he saw fit, though he knew that his changes would not be taken lightly; his revisions of break and lunchtime policies nearly got him into a[n] _____ with angry workers, who felt that they had been wronged.

From the list below, supply the words needed to complete the paragraph. Some words will not be used.

rife	nonchalant	donnybrook	interlocutor
contemptuous	nomenclature	brigand	

2. The _____ sprang from the hedges, produced his saber, and ordered the obviously wealthy couple to surrender their valuables, but the couple's _____ reaction to the threat bewildered the thief.

    "How _____ you aristocrats are," said the robber. "An outlaw threatens your lives, and you just stare with indifference?"

    "Yes, because they have nothing to fear. Lower your weapon, highwayman." The sudden voice of a new _____ startled the thief, but not as much as the sharp tip of the dagger jabbing into his shoulder blade. The thief dropped his sword, regreting he had not seen the watchman approaching from behind. To reduce the crime that had become _____ in the district, the king had recruited extra officers to patrol the cobblestone streets.

From the list below, supply the words needed to complete the paragraph. Some words will not be used.

stygian	brigand	incantation	cosmopolitan
carte blanche	nomenclature	sophistry	

3. In an effort to overcome the overwhelming boredom of his _____, stone-floored prison cell, Tobias exercised his knowledge by identifying each insect he saw by its Latin _____. The only alternative was to listen to the prisoner in the neighboring cell shout the same _____ that had failed to convince the judge that he was innocent. In several weeks, the repetitive, daily rant began to sound like a[n] _____ to Tobias, perhaps a spell that would melt the bars of the noisy prisoner's cell. The two prisoners conversed occasionally. Tobias, a well-traveled, renowned explorer, related tales from his _____ life, but the conversation inevitably returned to the topic of the other man's wrongful imprisonment.

EXERCISE II—Sentence Completion

Complete the sentence in a way that shows you understand the meaning of the italicized vocabulary word.

1. The *brigands* plotted to rob the train by…

2. Paul experienced a total *metamorphosis* in his behavior after…

3. The *contemptuous* child wondered why none of his classmates…

4. A *donnybrook* erupted at the grocery store when…

5. Many people know that H_2O is the *nomenclature* for…

6. The fans in the home crowd yelled a hilarious *incantation* when…

7. The *procrustean* bus driver refused to…

8. The *stygian* cave made a good hideout for the outlaw because…

9. Kelly thought herself too *cosmopolitan* to…

10. The lawn is *rife* with weeds this year because…

11. The cement foundation, overgrown with weeds, and littered with charred wood, is the only remaining *vestige* of...

12. George was a great *interlocutor* in the debate because he...

13. Ian had *carte blanche* when using the family car until he...

14. Try to remain *nonchalant* and avoid looking desperate when we ask...

15. The arch villain used *sophistry* to convince the hero to...

EXERCISE III—Roots, Prefixes, and Suffixes

Study the entries and answer the questions that follow.

The suffix *escent* means "becoming" or "growing."
The prefix *ob* means "toward" or "against."
The prefix *con* means "totally" or "completely."
The root *val* means "strong" or "healthy."
The root *rub* means "red."
The roots *irid* and *iris* mean "rainbow" or "brightly colored."
The root *fac* means "make."

1. *Using literal translations as guidance, define the following words without using a dictionary.*

   A. rubefacient
   B. iridescent
   C. rubescent
   D. convalescent
   E. iris
   F. valor

2. What do you think the musical term *crescendo* means?

3. List some of the deeds that a *valiant* knight might do.

4. List as many words as you can think of that contain the root *val*.

EXERCISE IV—Inference

Complete the sentences by inferring information about the italicized word from its context.

1. The forest around the house is *rife* with poison ivy, so we should...

2. Mike used to be rebellious, but he experienced a *metamorphosis* that...

3. If Nina behaved in a *nonchalant* manner when she saw her report card, then she probably...

EXERCISE V—Critical Reading

Below is a reading passage followed by several multiple-choice questions similar to the ones you will encounter on the SAT. Carefully read the passage and choose the best answer to each of the questions.

Edward Sanford Martin (1856-1939) was a humor writer and one of the founders of Life Magazine. The following passage is an excerpt from Martin's essay, "The Tyranny of Things." In the essay, Martin discusses how easily people become slaves to material goods, including even material things that are thought to be beneficial or coveted, such as large homes.

There was a story in the newspapers the other day about a Massachusetts minister who resigned his charge because someone had given his parish a fine house,
and his parishioners wanted him to live in it. His salary was too small, he said, to
admit of his living in a big house, and he would not do it. He was even deaf to the
5   proposal that he should share the proposed tenement with the sewing societies
and clubs of his church, and when the matter came to a serious issue, he relin-
quished his charge and sought a new field of usefulness. The situation was an
amusing instance of the embarrassment of riches. Let no one to whom restricted
quarters may have grown irksome, and who covets larger dimensions of shelter, be
10 too hasty in deciding that the minister was wrong. Did you ever see the house that
Hawthorne lived in at Lenox? Did you ever see Emerson's house at Concord? They
are good houses for Americans to know and remember. They permitted thought.
A big house is one of the greediest cormorants which can light upon a little
income. Backs may go threadbare and stomachs may worry along on indifferent
15 filling, but a house *will* have things, though its occupants go without. It is rarely
complete, and constantly tempts the imagination to flights in brick and dreams in
lath and plaster. It develops annual thirsts for paint and wallpaper, at least, if not
for marble and woodcarving. The plumbing in it must be kept in order on pain of
death. Whatever price is put on coal, it has to be heated in winter; and if it is rural

20   or suburban, the grass about it must be cut even though funerals in the family
have to be put off for the mowing. If the tenants are not rich enough to hire people
to keep their house clean, they must do it themselves, for there is no excuse that
will pass among housekeepers for a dirty house. The master of a house too big for
him may expect to spend the leisure which might be made intellectually or spiri-
25   tually profitable, in acquiring and putting into practice fag ends of the arts of the
plumber, the bell-hanger, the locksmith, the gas-fitter, and the carpenter. Presently
he will know how to do everything that can be done in the house, except enjoy
himself. He will learn about taxes, too, and water-rates, and how such abomina-
tions as sewers or new pavements are always liable to accrue at his expense. As for
30   the mistress, she will be a slave to carpets and curtains, wallpaper, painters, and
women who come in by the day to clean. She will be lucky if she gets a chance to
say her prayers, and thrice and four times happy when she can read a book or visit
with her friends. To live in a big house may be a luxury, provided that one has a
full set of money and an enthusiastic housekeeper in one's family; but to scrimp in
35   a big house is a miserable business. Yet such is human folly, that for a man to
refuse to live in a house because it is too big for him, is such an exceptional exhibition of sense that it becomes the favorite paragraph of a day in the newspapers.

     An ideal of earthly comfort, so common that every reader must have seen it, is
to get a house so big that it is burdensome to maintain, and fill it up so full of gim-
40   cracks that it is a constant occupation to keep it in order. Then, when the expense
of living in it is so great that you can't afford to go away and rest from the burden
of it, the situation is complete and boarding houses and cemeteries begin to yawn
for you. How many Americans, do you suppose, out of the droves that flock annu-
ally to Europe, are running away from oppressive houses?

45   When nature undertakes to provide a house, it fits the occupant. Animals which
build by instinct build only what they need, but man's building instinct, if it gets
a chance to spread itself at all, is boundless, just as all his instincts are. For it is
man's peculiarity that nature has filled him with impulses to do things, and left it
to his discretion when to stop. She never tells him when he has finished. And per-
50   haps we ought not to be surprised that in so many cases it happens that he does
not know, but just goes ahead as long as the materials last.

     If another *man* tries to oppress him, he understands that and is ready to fight to
death and sacrifice all he has, rather than submit; but the tyranny of *things* is so
subtle, so gradual in its approach, and comes so masked with seeming benefits,
55   that it has him hopelessly bound before he suspects his fetters. He says from day
to day, "I will add thus to my house;" "I will have one or two more horses;" "I will
make a little greenhouse in my garden;" "I will allow myself the luxury of another hired man;" and so he goes on having things and imagining that he is richer for
them. Presently he begins to realize that it is the things that own him. He has piled
60   them up on his shoulders, and there they sit like Sinbad's Old Man and drive him;
and it becomes a daily question whether he can keep his trembling legs or not.

     All of which is not meant to prove that property has no real value, or to rebut
Charles Lamb's scornful denial that enough is as good as a feast. It is not meant to
apply to the rich, who can have things comfortably, if they are philosophical; but
65   to us poor, who have constant need to remind ourselves that where the verbs *to
have* and *to be* cannot both be completely inflected, the verb *to be* is the one that
best repays concentration.

1. The tone of this passage is best described as
   A. cynical.
   B. supportive.
   C. forlorn.
   D. evasive.
   E. supercilious.

2. As used in the first paragraph, *charge* most nearly means
   A. accusation.
   B. debt.
   C. ridicule.
   D. duty.
   E. shock.

3. According to the context of the first paragraph, Emerson and Hawthorne's houses were probably
   A. elaborate and expansive.
   B. practical, plain residences.
   C. constructed more than 200 years ago.
   D. larger than the homes of their neighbors.
   E. simple tents with dirt floors.

4. The *cormorants* in line 13 are probably
   A. strike-anywhere matches.
   B. feelings of doubt.
   C. boulders.
   D. bands of robbers.
   E. voracious sea birds.

5. Which choice is the best interpretation of the following quotation?

   > "Backs may go threadbare and stomachs may worry
   > along on indifferent filling, but a house *will* have things,
   > though its occupants go without."

   A. The maintenance of a house always takes priority over the people living in it, even if they are forced to go without proper food or clothing.
   B. It's a bad time to buy real estate because interest rates are rising and the price of food and clothing is increasing.
   C. The best house is one that includes a butler and a full wardrobe.
   D. No matter how much money someone has, a house will ensure that he or she will not be able to afford to eat or buy clothing.
   E. People inevitably spend too much money on their homes.

6. According to paragraph 2, there is nothing wrong with living in a large house if
   A. the house contains no decorations or furniture.
   B. the occupants are familiar with tax laws, painting, and mowing grass.
   C. the occupants have plenty of money and someone to maintain the house.
   D. the house is not in need of repairs.
   E. the occupants have no friends.

7. As used in line 34, *scrimp* most nearly means
   A. to live.
   B. to economize.
   C. to repair.
   D. to eat.
   E. to spend freely.

8. According to the author, people such as the minister are accused of having an "embarrassment of riches" because
   A. few people understand why someone would refuse to live in a large house.
   B. the house offered to the minister is bedecked with fine woodwork.
   C. everyone wants a larger house than the one he or she currently owns.
   D. ministers generally have few possessions, so wealth embarrasses them.
   E. a modest, wealthy person would never accept a free house.

9. Which choice best paraphrases the following quotation?

    > "but to us poor, who have constant need to remind
    > ourselves that where the verbs *to have* and *to be* can-
    > not both be completely inflected, the verb *to be* is the
    > one that best repays concentration."

    A. Those who cannot be happy simply existing, or "being," become
        disillusioned by "wanting" all the time.
    B. The poor, who need more than they want, are usually happier to
        think about what kind of people they are.
    C. Material possessions are nothing compared to those things that
        define a person.
    D. The poor, who cannot claim to have or have had material things, are
        better off considering "what they are" than "what they have."
    E. Wealthy people, who know who they are and what they want, have
        little need to worry about owning a large house.

10. Which of the following statements best supports the theme of this passage?
    A. Large houses require a lot of work.
    B. A free house, small or large, is always better than no house.
    C. People become slaves to their material possessions.
    D. Being wealthy and owning a small house is a ridiculous situation.
    E. Large families should reconsider whether they require large homes.

Lesson Three

1. **scapegoat** (skāp´ gōt) *n.* one who bears the blame for others
    Andy was frequently absent, so other workers made him the *scapegoat* for their own mistakes.
    syn: patsy; sucker

2. **peremptory** (pə remp´ tə rē) *adj.* not allowing refusal or delay; imperative
    The guard issued a *peremptory* warning to step away from the fence or be fired upon.
    syn: authoritative; unconditional   *ant: roundabout; passive; equivocal*

3. **atelier** (a təl yā´) n. an artist's or a designer's workshop
    The painter converted his garage into an *atelier* to work on his creative masterpieces.

4. **axiom** (ak´ sē əm) *n.* a universal truth; an established rule
    According to some people, the most important *axiom* of all is, "Do unto others as you would have them do unto you."
    syn: fundamental; theorem   *ant: absurdity*

5. **dulcet** (dul´ sit) *adj.* melodious; pleasing to the ear
    The opera singer's *dulcet* voice earned her a prominent place in the upcoming production.
    syn: harmonic; melodic   *ant: cacophonous; dissonant*

6. **usurp** (yōō sûrp´) *v.* to take over; to seize power
    The evil heir planned to *usurp* the throne while the king was ill.
    syn: commandeer; seize; co-opt   *ant: abdicate; relinquish*

7. **patronizing** (pā´ trə nīz ing) *adj.* treating with condescension; acting superior
    Despite his *patronizing* treatment of the employees, the foreman was still well liked.
    syn: lofty; arrogant   *ant: humble; friendly*

8. **iniquity** (i nik´ wi tē) *n.* an evil or wicked act
    He heartily repented his *iniquity,* but only after he faced a lifelong prison sentence.
    syn: abomination; injustice; sin

9. **archaic** (är kā´ ik) *adj.* no longer current or applicable; antiquated
    Some states still have *archaic* laws that regulate horse-and-buggy traffic.
    syn: obsolete; outmoded   *ant: current; modern*

10. **vacillate** (vas´ ə lāt) *v.* to waver; to sway indecisively
    For years Bobby *vacillated* between liking one band and then another.
    syn: fluctuate; swing; waffle   *ant: decide*

11. **perspicacious** (pûr spi kā´ shəs) *adj.* keen; mentally sharp
    The *perspicacious* gambler knew that he would need to make a hasty exit
    after winning most of the cowboys' money.
    syn: shrewd; keen; clever   *ant: dull; stupid*

12. **abstemious** (ab stē´ mē əs) *adj.* using or consuming sparingly
    Bill, who wants to lose weight, is *abstemious* in eating foods high in fat.
    syn: frugal; moderate   *ant: gluttonous; greedy*

13. **talisman** (tal´ is mən) *n.* a magic charm or superstitious object for
    protection or luck
    The wizard claimed that no harm would come to anyone holding the
    talisman.

14. **expurgate** (ek´ spər gāt) *v.* to remove vulgar or objectionable material
    Censors sometimes feel that it is necessary to *expurgate* offensive
    scenes from movies.
    syn: censor; bowdlerize; sanitize

15. **pellucid** (pə lōō´ sid) *adj.* transparent; clear
    Eliminate extraneous words if you want your paper to have a *pellucid*
    message.
    syn: limpid   *ant: obscure; opaque*

EXERCISE I—Words in Context

*From the list below, supply the words needed to complete the paragraph. Some
words will not be used.*

usurp	atelier	pellucid	archaic
axiom	dulcet	iniquity	

1.   "I prefer to think of this factory as a giant _____, where a team of
artists creates not specialized tools, but hand-machined works of art," said
Roger, the owner of Calumette Industries. "And as long as our goal remains
_____ to every employee, this company will soar." Roger, who took
over the failing operation just months ago, sparked life back into the floundering plant by replacing _____ industry practices with new methods guaranteed to increase production; however, despite Roger's many
changes to the plant, he was quick to note that he is a firm believer in the
_____, "Don't fix things that aren't broken."
    During a tour of the factory one could see by the smile on Roger's face
that the repetitive clanging of electric motors and hydraulic presses was
_____ music to the industrialist's ears.

*From the list below, supply the words needed to complete the paragraph. Some
words will not be used.*

scapegoat	atelier	iniquity	vacillated
perspicacious	expurgate	talisman	

2.   When an obscene photograph appeared in the school yearbook, the
administration immediately sought a[n] _____ to take the blame for
the _____. Angry students and parents blamed Dora, the yearbook
editor, for not being _____ enough to have spotted the photo before
the book was sent to the printer. Now, the school must collect the books
and return them to the printer to _____ the photograph. Dora, a jun-
ior, _____ over whether she would sign up for the yearbook staff
again next year.

From the list below, supply the words needed to complete the paragraph. Some words will not be used.

talisman	archaic	abstemious	scapegoat
patronizing	usurp	peremptory	

3.   Paranoid that someone would _____ control of his latest project, Bob carried the scale model of the building with him all around the office as though it were some kind of _____ that would protect him from any dragons hiding in the cubicles. Some of the employees giggled when Bob walked by, and others gave him _____ looks, which made him feel like a fearful toddler carrying a security blanket. Mrs. Simmons, the manager, began to worry that perhaps Bob was stressed out, so she called a meeting with him. During the meeting, the manager reminded Bob that his _____ use of vacation time was not healthy; he absolutely must get away from the office for a little while. Two weeks later, as Bob basked in the Caribbean sun, he wished that the boss would have prescribed a[n] _____ vacation months earlier.

EXERCISE II—Sentence Completion

Complete the sentence in a way that shows you understand the meaning of the italicized vocabulary word.

1. Chris knew that he would become the *scapegoat* if the police learned that he...

2. Uncle Pete thought that carrying a *talisman*, such as a rabbit's foot, would...

3. Catherine feared that someone would try to *usurp* her position at the company if she...

4. Virgil got lost in the city because his *archaic* map did not...

5. The gymnasium was once open to the public, but owing to the *iniquities* of a few vandals, it is now...

6. To ensure that Adam had a *pellucid* idea of what she was explaining, Sheila...

7. During the bomb scare, the principal issued a *peremptory* order to...

8. The *patronizing* babysitter told the children...

9. Occasionally, Lisa strayed from her *abstemious* budget in order to...

10. In his *atelier*, the carpenter...

11. At the store, Susan *vacillated* over which...

12. To *expurgate* the graffiti sprayed on the walls of the tunnel, the cleanup crew...

13. The fugitive would have escaped if a *perspicacious* citizen had not noticed...

14. While camping, Liz quickly fell asleep to the *dulcet* sound of...

15. Jerry often muttered the *axiom*, "If you want something done right, do it yourself," when...

EXERCISE III—Roots, Prefixes, and Suffixes

Study the entries and answer the questions that follow.

The root *ratio* means "reason."
The root *ment* means "mind."
The root *gno* means "knowledge."
The prefix *de* means "away."
The prefix *ir* means "not."
The prefix *a* means "without."
The prefix *pro* means "before" or "in advance."

1. *Using literal translations as guidance, define the following words without using a dictionary.*

   A. prognosticate   D. mentality
   B. agnostic   E. rationale
   C. irrational   F. dementia

2. Explain the difference between a *ratio* and a *ration*.

3. What do you think a *mentalist* does?

4. If *dia* means "through," or "by way of," what does the word *diagnosis* mean literally?

5. List as many words as you can think of that contain the root *ratio*.

EXERCISE IV—Inference

Complete the sentences by inferring information about the italicized word from its context.

1. During the drought, the mayor asked citizens to be *abstemious* in their water consumption because...

2. If an *archaic* computer system will not run the latest software, the user will need to...

3. The answer to the calculus problem was not yet *pellucid* to Jack, so he should...

EXERCISE V—Writing

Here is a writing prompt similar to the one you will find on the writing portion of the SAT.

Plan and write an essay based on the following statement:

I have never found a companion that was so companionable as solitude. We are for the most part more lonely when we go abroad among men than when we stay in our chambers. A man thinking or working is always alone, let him be where he will.

–Henry David Thoreau: *Walden*

Assignment: In an essay, explain whether being alone was a depressing or a pleasurable experience for Thoreau. Include an interpretation of the second sentence, about being lonely among other people, and explain why it supports your opinion as to Thoreau's perception of solitude. Support your position by discussing examples from literature, art, science, current events, or your own experience or observation.

Thesis: Write a one-sentence response to the above assignment. Make certain this sentence offers a clear statement of your position.

Example: Thoreau loved solitude because it is much easier to be at ease with oneself than among strangers, especially in a modern world in which selfishness and greed have become acceptable forms of inspiration.

Organizational Plan: If your thesis is the point on which you want to end, where does your essay need to begin? List the points of development that are inevitable in leading your reader from your beginning point to your end point. This list is your outline.

Draft: Use your thesis as both your beginning and your end. Following your outline, write a good first draft of your essay. Remember to support all of your points with examples, facts, references to reading, etc.

Review and revise: Exchange essays with a classmate. Using the scoring guide for Development on page 249, score your partner's essay (while he or she scores yours). Focus on the development of ideas and use of language conventions. If necessary, rewrite your essay to improve the development of ideas and/or your use of language.

Improving Paragraphs

Read the following passage and then answer the multiple-choice questions that follow. The questions will require you to make decisions regarding the revision of the reading selection.

(1) The world as we know it would not exist today if it were not for gigantic aircraft capable of carrying hundreds of tons of people, supplies, and equipment. (2) The credit for inspiring such aircraft must go to a versatile Texan by the name of Howard Hughes—the inventor of the first massive "flying boat" that most now remember as the "Spruce Goose."

(3) Howard Hughes was what most would describe as a Renaissance man. (4) He was an actor, a director, a theater owner, a pilot, and an engineer. (5) Though he never finished high school, Hughes attended classes at California Institute of Technology, thanks to a considerable donation by his father. (6) Hughes's father was wealthy. (7) Hughes's father died when Hughes was only eighteen years old. (8) A judge awarded Hughes legal adulthood just after his nineteenth birthday, which allowed the young man to take control of his father's estate from his uncle. (9) Part of the estate included Hughes Tool Company, and Hughes, taking advantage of the booming aircraft technology industry of the early twentieth century, formed the Hughes Aircraft Company division in 1932. (10) With this company and the help of famous shipbuilder Henry Kaiser, Hughes established a contract with the government to build three "flying boats." (11) Hughes never finished building three planes, but he did successfully complete one.

(12) To meet government specifications, Hughes's flying boat had to be capable of transporting cargo and men over long distances. (13) Enemies were destroying shipping lanes during World War II, and the military needed the flying boat to carry soldiers and supplies high above enemy ships and submarines. (14) The contract awarded Hughes eighteen million dollars to build the three aircraft, and Hughes added another seven million of his own fortune to fund the project. (15) With adequate funding and sheer determination, Hughes then proves to the world that human ingenuity could make a 200-ton pile of wood airborne.

(16) The public nicknamed the flying boat the "Spruce Goose" to mock Hughes for his apparent failure. (17) The flying boat was constructed of mostly birch wood (not spruce) and fabric. (18) It had a single hull, eight of the most powerful engines of the time, and a single vertical tail. (19) Hughes covered the primary control surfaces in fabric, and the rest of the plane was laminated birch. (20) The plane was a behemoth—the largest aircraft built in the era—with a 320-foot wingspan, a length of 219 feet, and a wing area of 11,430 square feet. (21) Most impressively, the flying boat could take off with a weight of 400,000 pounds, or 200 tons.

(22) Though the giant plane flew, it flew only once. (23) On November 2, 1947, well after the end of the war and in the midst of Congressional hearings to determine why the planes were not yet completed, Hughes returned to California to run supposed engine tests on his plane. (24) In the waters off Long Beach, Hughes took the controls, shoved the throttles to the stops, and, to the amazement of onlookers, the Spruce Goose took flight. (25) Hughes lifted the plane 70 feet from the ocean

and it lumbered along at 80 miles per hour for about a mile before making a perfect landing.

(26) Many historians claim that while Congress decided to cancel the contract for the H-4 Hercules, the short flight of the mammoth plane vindicated Howard Hughes. (27) The flying boat may have been late, but it was well ahead of its time; to this day, the Spruce Goose is, by wingspan, the largest plane ever built. (28) After the historic flight was made by Hughes, the plane was moved to its hanger and was stored and maintained as though active until 1980, four years after the death of Howard Hughes. (29) It now rests in Oregon as a colossal artifact at the Evergreen Aviation Museum. (30) Someday, perhaps, Hughes's invention will inspire a new generation of inventors to do what others say cannot be done.

1. Which sentence can be deleted from paragraph 2 without changing the intent of the paragraph?
    A. sentence 3
    B. sentence 4
    C. sentence 6
    D. sentence 7
    E. sentence 9

2. Which of the following corrects an error in sentence 15?
    A. Specify which type of engineering requires ingenuity.
    B. Rewrite the sentence to omit the comma splice.
    C. *Ingenuity* is plural and requires the plural verb *are*.
    D. Change *proves* to *proved*.
    E. Include a mention of World War II in the sentence.

3. Which sentence from paragraph 4 should be moved to paragraph 5?
    A. sentence 16
    B. sentence 17
    C. sentence 18
    D. sentence 19
    E. sentence 20

4. Which of the following suggestions would best improve sentence 28?
    A. Divide it into two separate sentences.
    B. Delete *four years after the death of Howard Hughes*.
    C. Change the sentence from the passive voice to the active voice.
    D. Move *After the historic flight was made by Hughes* to the end of the sentence.
    E. Delete *and was stored*.

5. Which revision would best clarify the term *H-4 Hercules* in sentence 6?
   A. Replace all references to Hughes's plane with *H-4 Hercules*.
   B. Mention the official name of the Spruce Goose earlier in the passage.
   C. Explain why the plane is named after a mythical person.
   D. Replace *H-4 Hercules* with *Spruce Goose*.
   E. Replace *H-4 Hercules* with *Flying Boat*.

Lesson Four

1. **efficacious** (ef i kā´ shəs) *adj.* effective; producing the desired outcome
   The shot of adrenaline was *efficacious* in restarting the victim's heart.
   syn: productive; useful   *ant: ineffective*

2. **catharsis** (kə thär´ sis) *n.* a release of emotional tension
   The movie lacked a *catharsis* because the villain received no punishment.
   syn: purgation

3. **inundate** (in´ un dāt) *v.* to overwhelm; to fill beyond capacity
   Callers *inundated* the radio station with requests for the popular new song.
   syn: flood; overwhelm

4. **revere** (ri vîr´) *v.* to regard with respect, awe, or adoration
   Alexander the Great's soldiers *revered* their leader because he led the troops into every battle.
   syn: venerate; respect; honor   *ant: revile*

5. **internecine** (in tər ne´ sēn) *adj.* mutually destructive
   The *internecine* battle resulted in thousands of casualties, but neither side gained new land.
                                        ant: constructive; beneficial

6. **risible** (ri´ zə bəl) *adj.* relating to laughter; laughable
   The *risible* statement made by the gentleman in the front row was completely ridiculous, but it was amusing.
   syn: comical; jocular; jocund   *ant: grave; solemn*

7. **sybaritic** (si bə rit´ ik) *adj.* marked by luxury or pleasure
   Ice sculptures, massive chandeliers, and live entertainment were commonplace at Loren's *sybaritic* parties.
   syn: luxurious; ostentatious; grandiose   *ant: modest; simple; plain*

8. **crepuscular** (kri pus´ kyə lər) *adj.* pertaining to twilight
   That species of trout has *crepuscular* feeding habits, so you'll catch the most at daybreak or sunset.

9. **kudos*** (kōō´ dōz) *n.* acclaim or praise
   The director of the successful new musical won *kudos* from most critics.
   syn: honor; distinction   *ant: disapproval; rejection*
   Kudos always takes a singular verb

10. **estrange** (i stränj´) *v.* to alienate
    Jill's overbearing mother-in-law *estranged* Jill from her husband.
    syn: disaffect; antagonize   *ant: unite; endear*

11. **intrinsic** (in trin´ sik) *adj.* of or relating to a thing's basic nature;
    inherent
    Humans have an *intrinsic* desire to be loved.
    syn: basic; elemental; inborn   *ant: extrinsic*

12. **maxim** (mak´ sim) *n.* an established principle; a truth or rule of
    conduct
    The coach frequently spoke the *maxim*, "A chain is only as strong as its
    weakest link."
    syn: axiom; apothegm; proverb

13. **putrid** (pū´ trid) *adj.* rotten and foul smelling
    We rolled up the car windows to escape the *putrid* smell of a dead skunk
    on the road.
    syn: fetid; rancid; malodorous   *ant: aromatic; fragrant*

14. **servile** (sûr´ vīl) *adj.* submissive; slavish
    The *servile* dog cowered before its intimidating master.
    syn: subservient; ignoble   *ant: haughty; domineering*

15. **apocryphal** (ə pok´ rə fəl) *adj.* of questionable authenticity, but
    widely believed
    Modern historians dismiss the *apocryphal* story that George Washington
    cut down a cherry tree.
    syn: dubious; equivocal; spurious   *ant: genuine; authentic*

EXERCISE I—Words in Context

From the list below, supply the words needed to complete the paragraph. Some words will not be used.

     sybaritic   crepuscular   apocryphal   servile
     maxim   internecine   estrange

1.   When Johnny turned fifteen, he inexplicably began a[n] _____ war with his parents. The Smiths asked Johnny how he was able to afford his new laptop computer, and Johnny gave them a[n] _____ story about how it had fallen from the back of a truck. Enraged, they confiscated the computer and ordered Johnny to sit and listen.

        "When your luck runs out and you end up in prison, it will _____ you from your family and friends, and it will limit your options for the future! Your grades are already suffering, and if you make a criminal record for yourself, you'll end up having a[n] _____ job with long hours and lousy pay while your successful friends enjoy _____ lifestyles by comparison. Is that what you want?"

From the list below, supply the words needed to complete the paragraph. Some words will not be used.

     estrange   efficacious   crepuscular   risible
     kudos   inundate   intrinsic

2.   Amy arrived at the empty lot just before sundown, when the _____ animals began to emerge from the forest to feed in the grassy field. The new development would soon ruin the _____ value of Amy's childhood stomping grounds, so she wanted to enjoy it one last time before the construction crews arrived. Amy looked over the rows of beech trees and clusters of mountain laurel and thought of the many _____ lessons she had learned there as a child; for example, that poison ivy should not be added to books of pressed leaves. The visit _____ Amy with childhood memories; she would miss having such a[n] _____ way to forget about her many grown-up responsibilities.

From the list below, supply the words needed to complete the paragraph. Some words will not be used.

catharsis	putrid	efficacious	maxim
kudos	internecine	revere	

3.　　The young captain earned _____ for leading several successful missions in the past, but his troops did not _____ him when he ordered them to march through the _____ mud of a swamp during the most recent training mission. If anyone complained, the captain simply repeated the _____, "We sweat in peace so that we don't bleed in war."

What many of the soldiers didn't realize was that the captain had planned this rigorous training mission as a[n] _____ to relieve the tension of living in the confining barracks in the months prior to the troops' deployment.

EXERCISE II—Sentence Completion

Complete the sentence in a way that shows you understand the meaning of the italicized vocabulary word.

1. The *servile* intern withheld any complaints when the cable television magnate told him to...

2. The inspirational posters in the guidance counselor's office listed *maxims* about...

3. Most urban legends are *apocryphal* tales simply meant to...

4. Customers *inundated* the department store when...

5. The *sybaritic* main cabin of the gigantic yacht has all the pleasures of...

6. The company needed an *efficacious* advertising campaign in order to...

7. The antique watch had little material value, but it had enormous *intrinsic* worth because...

8. A hobby or physical activity in the evening can be a pleasant *catharsis* for people who...

9. Barb enjoyed *kudos* from her coworkers after she...

10. When the wind blows just the right way, the *putrid* stench of...

11. *Crepuscular* wildlife emerged from the forest just before...

12. Jody *estranged* herself from her family when she...

13. Sergeant Butters didn't *revere* the general well enough to volunteer for...

14. Except for one *risible* scene during the opening credits, the movie...

15. Roy has an *internecine* philosophy that when someone is wronged, he or she should...

EXERCISE III—Roots, Prefixes, and Suffixes

Study the entries and answer the questions that follow.

The root *cant* means "sing."
The root *clam* means "shout."
The prefix *in* means "in," "on," or "onto."
The prefix *re* means "back."
The prefix *ad* means "toward."
The prefix *de* means "down from."
The suffix *ment* means "result of."

1. Using literal translations as guidance, define the following words without using a dictionary.

    A. acclamation   D. incantation
    B. chant   E. canticle
    C. clamorous   F. declamation

2. If *ex* means "out," then the word _____ means "to shout out suddenly."

3. The famous poem by Dante entitled *The Divine Comedy* is divided into chapters called *cantos*. How do you suppose the chapters got this name?

4. The word *enchantment* is also formed with the root *cant*. If *en* means "into," what is the literal definition of this word?

5. List as many words as you can think of that contain the prefix *de*.

EXERCISE IV—Inference

Complete the sentences by inferring information about the italicized word from its context.

1. If doctors are pleased that Gary's operation proved *efficacious*, then the procedure...

2. Your friends will avoid you if you *estrange* them by...

3. During the trial, a judge will usually dismiss *apocryphal* evidence because...

EXERCISE V—Critical Reading

Below is a pair of reading passages followed by several multiple-choice questions similar to the ones you will encounter on the SAT. Carefully read both passages and choose the best answer to each of the questions.

The following passages describe circumstances surrounding the lives of two different young rulers. Alexandrina Victoria, Queen of the United Kingdom of Britain and Empress of India, ruled from 1837 until 1901. Alexander the Great, King of Macedonia, constructed the largest western empire of the ancient world during his reign from 336 to 323 B.C.

Passage 1

In 1792, the French overthrew King Louis XVI and his wife, Marie Antoinette, and sparked three decades of conquest and bloodshed under the new French Republic and the imperial designs of Napoleon. After Napoleon was finally silenced at the battle of Waterloo in 1815, the Congress of Vienna restored monarchy in
5   France. Meanwhile, King George III, the "mad king" of England, neared the end of a sixty-year reign, the latter part of which was marked by bouts of insanity. When Queen Victoria was born in 1819, the continent of Europe was breathing a collective sigh of relief.

Victoria grew up during the reigns of her uncles, King George IV and King
10   William IV; however, her mother, who scorned the immoral lives of William and especially George, ensured that Victoria had little exposure to the court lives of the two monarchs. When William died in 1837, the eighteen-year-old Victoria found herself Queen. As one might expect from an ambitious teenager, Victoria quickly shrugged off her mother's domineering influence; however, Victoria had but a frac-
15   tion of the power of previous English monarchs: the Reform Act of 1832 had delegated executive power to a committee comprising members of the House of Commons. After 1832, the role of a monarch in the creation of policy was little more than that of an advisor who was capable of swaying public opinion if necessary.

20   The Reform Act, combined with Victoria's image of honesty and modesty, helped to protect England from the types of upheavals that plagued the rest of Europe at the time. The French revolted in 1830 and then again in 1848, the same year in which revolution wracked Prussia and the Austro-Hungarian Empire. The *Communist Manifesto* appeared also in 1848, and the philosophy therein served as
25   the inspiration for revolts around the world for the next century.

England enjoyed a period of relative stability while revolutionary passions ran their course through the rest of the world. In 1840, Queen Victoria married her cousin Prince Albert, and Albert introduced a conservative tone into English politics and society. Albert insisted upon a strict code of conduct in court, and he urged
30   Victoria to voice her opinions among members of the executive cabinet. Under Albert's guidance, Victoria demonstrated increasingly conservative politics during

an era that saw the birth of tradition-challenging ideas such as nationalism, liber-alism, democracy, and socialism.

35   By the time Queen Victoria died in 1901, the British Empire had added India to its territorial holdings and survived the turmoil and bloodshed concomitant with the revolutions and the creation of two new nations, Germany and Italy, on the European Continent. The anxieties of a teenage queen could easily have sent the British public into a panic, but Victoria's inborn strength and aplomb brought sta-bility and security to her nation, and they made Queen Victoria one of the most
40   revered monarchs in British history.

Passage 2

The father of Alexander the Great, Philip of Macedon, had conquered all of Greece before his assassination in 336 B.C. When Philip died, he left twenty-year-old Alexander with the small task of conquering the Persian Empire. Like a flare that burns with an intense, white-hot flame, Alexander the Great lived fiercely but
5   died young, at the age of thirty-two; however, in his twelve years as king, Alexander built an empire that stretched from Egypt to China.

One may wonder what type of childhood and adolescent influences must have been at work to create such a powerful ruler. At first glance, Alexander was any-thing but a charismatic leader—he is described as having been of average appear-
10   ance and of nervous temperament. His one outstanding feature is said to have been his piercing gaze.

Much legend has arisen around Alexander's childhood. He is said to have received a group of envoys from Persia on a day when his father was reviewing his troops, and to have made a more favorable impression on them than his father
15   would have—at the age of six!

Alexander's first teacher, Leonidas, ingrained his own ascetic personality in young Alexander. He imparted a strong work ethic to the boy, which gave Alexander the self-discipline he needed to be a good soldier and a young king. When Alexander traveled with his armies, he lived as his soldiers lived, sleeping on
20   the ground and sharing unsavory rations, foregoing extravagant tents, regal vest-ments, and luxurious meals that had no purpose on the battlefield.

Alexander's second teacher, Lysimacuis, taught Alexander to appreciate the arts of music, poetry, and drama, but his most famous teacher, the Athenian philoso-pher Aristotle, passed along his knowledge of science, medicine, philosophy, ethics,
25   and politics, all of which contributed to the background that would soon make the thirteen-year-old Alexander a great leader and champion of his people.

One story that demonstrates young Alexander's precocious nature is that of Alexander and his horse, Bucephalus. Philoneicus of Thessaly presented a horse to sell to Philip, but none of Philip's farmhands could handle the wild Bucephalus.
30   Alexander noticed that the animal was afraid of its own shadow, so he wagered 13 talents—the price of the horse—that he could tame it. Philip accepted the wager, and Alexander quickly collected his prize after leading the horse toward the sun, so that the animal could not see its shadow, mounting it, and riding it.

Not all of the tales associated with Alexander's youth are as charming as that of

35 the tale of Bucephalus. Philip took several concubines during his reign, one of whom was Cleopatra, the daughter of a Macedonian aristocrat. During the wedding feast, Cleopatra's uncle, Attalus, suggested that Philip and Cleopatra produce a pure Macedonian heir (Alexander's mother, Olympias, was an Albanian who practiced Dionysian rituals that were not commonly condoned in Macedonia; Alexander was
40 not considered to be a pure Macedonian). Alexander took great offense to the suggestion, a brawl ensued, and a rift grew between Alexander and his father that lasted until Philip was assassinated in 336.

Alexander is often described as the ruler who accomplished more in thirteen years than anyone else had accomplished in an entire lifetime. Alexander, like
45 many princes, had a superior education in arts, sciences, and military strategy, but perhaps it was the unconventional education—that which a dysfunctional family presents—that somehow fueled Alexander's ambition. Whatever the deciding factors, Alexander undoubtedly remains among the most powerful military leaders in the history of the world.

1. The personification used in line 7 of the first passage is used to
   A. describe the mental state of King George III.
   B. demonstrate the purpose of the Congress of Vienna.
   C. express the mood of Europe in 1815.
   D. assess the political climate of England in the early 1800s.
   E. portray the conflict between Victoria's mother and Victoria's uncles.

2. According to passage 1, which is the most likely reason for the Reform Act of 1832?
   A. the modesty demonstrated by the young Queen Victoria
   B. the instability encountered under King George III and his two brothers
   C. the French Revolution of 1830
   D. the writing of *The Communist Manifesto*
   E. the immoral conduct of the English royal court

3. The best title for the first passage would be
   A. European Revolutions during the Reign of Queen Victoria.
   B. The Benefits of the Reform Act of 1832.
   C. England from King George to Communism.
   D. England: An Oasis of Stability in Nineteenth-Century Europe.
   E. The Expansion of the British Empire.

4. As used in line 35 of passage one, *concomitant* most nearly means
   A. accompanying.
   B. sympathetic.
   C. contradictory.
   D. necessary.
   E. ancillary.

5. Which word would be the best antonym for *ascetic* as it appears in line 16 of passage 2?
   A. Spartan
   B. cynical
   C. austere
   D. cheap
   E. indulgent

6. According to passage 2, which of the following was probably NOT a factor in the development of Alexander's personality?
   A. Philip's dislike of Olympias' religious beliefs
   B. Leonidas' belief in the denial of the self
   C. Alexander's skill with horses
   D. Philip's polygamous practices
   E. Aristotle's teachings in ethics

7. As used in line 20 of passage 2, *vestments* most nearly means
   A. robes.
   B. weaponry.
   C. goblets.
   D. scrolls.
   E. attitudes.

8. The best title for passage 2 would be
   A. An Ambassador at Age Six.
   B. An Imperialistic Mind.
   C. Legends of Alexander's Youth.
   D. The Youth of a Warrior King.
   E. Aristotle and Alexander.

9. Which of the following statements is NOT true about the two passages?
   A. Passage 2 is more skeptical than passage 1.
   B. Passage 1 is more patriotic than passage 2.
   C. Passage 2 is written more for an academic audience than passage 1.
   D. Passage 2 is biographical, while passage 1 is historical.
   E. Passage 2 focuses on psychology more than Passage 1.

10. Which choice best describes the tone of each passage?
    A. Passage 1 is cynical, and passage 2 is pedantic.
    B. Passage 1 is patriotic, and passage 2 is scholarly.
    C. Passage 1 is pompous, and passage 2 is strident.
    D. Passage 1 is bombastic, and passage 2 is ironic.
    E. Passage 1 is studious, and passage 2 is informal.

Lesson Five

1. **consternation** (kon stər nā´ shən) *n.* alarming dismay or concern
   The announcement of a pop quiz caused *consternation* among the students.
   syn: bewilderment; shock; trepidation   *ant: composure; tranquility*

2. **anomaly** (ə nom´ ə lē) *n.* a deviation from the norm; an odd or peculiar occurrence
   The sailor immediately notified the captain when he saw an *anomaly* on the sonar screen.
   syn: eccentricity; irregularity; oddity

3. **vitriolic** (vit rē ol´ ik) *adj.* harsh in tone; bitterly critical
   The critic's *vitriolic* review of the new film prompted thousands of contradictory letters.
   syn: caustic; offensive; scathing   *ant: flattering; genial*

4. **preamble** (prē´ am bəl) *n.* a preliminary statement; an introduction
   After reciting a long-winded *preamble*, the lawyer finally presented some pertinent facts.
   syn: prologue; preface; opening   *ant: epilogue; finale*

5. **coterie** (kō´ tə rē) *n.* a small group of people who share interests and meet frequently
   Virginia Woolf was a member of the Bloomsbury Group, a *coterie* of English authors respected for its talent, but ridiculed for its arrogance.
   syn: circle; clique; society

6. **expiate** (ek´ spē āt) *v.* to make amends for
   Johnny mowed the neighbors' lawn free of charge all summer to *expiate* his breaking their front window with a baseball.
   syn: atone; correct; rectify

7. **compendium** (kəm pen´ dē əm) *n.* a list or collection of items
   Jen perused a *compendium* of antique toys to find the value of an old doll.
   syn: compilation; index; anthology

8. **comprise** (kəm prīz´) *v.* to include or consist of; contain
   Canada *comprises* ten provinces and three territories.
   syn: constitute; encompass; incorporate   *ant: exclude; lack*

9. **eidetic** (ī det´ ik) *adj.* pertaining to extraordinarily detailed and vivid recall
   The author attempted to describe the *eidetic* scenes in his head.
   syn: vivid   *ant: vague*

10. **innocuous** (i nok´ yōō əs) *adj.* harmless
    The assassin wore a disguise and a smile to make himself look like an *innocuous* old man.
    syn: inoffensive; innocent   *ant: injurious*

11. **foist** (foist) *v.* to pass off as genuine or valuable
    The secret service arrested the man who *foisted* counterfeit $20 bills off on the unsuspecting country.
    syn: fob

12. **plethora** (pleth´ ər ə) *n.* an overabundance; excess
    The library has a *plethora* of information about most any subject imaginable.
    syn: surplus   *ant: deficiency; shortage; paucity*

13. **flippancy** (flip´ ənt cē) *n.* disrespect
    His *flippancy* in class often got him sent to the principal's office.
    syn: irreverence; rudeness; impertinence   *ant: respect; reverence*

14. **incongruous** (in kong´ grōō əs) *adj.* incompatible; unsuitable for the situation
    Ed's *incongruous* joke about policemen ensured he would get a speeding ticket.
    syn: discordant; improper   *ant: compatible; fitting*

15. **disconcert** (dis kən sûrt´) *v.* to frustrate; confuse
    The lengthy calculus problem on the quiz *disconcerted* Nancy.
    syn: agitate; fluster; perplex   *ant: enlighten; comfort; encourage*

EXERCISE I—Words in Context

From the list below, supply the words needed to complete the paragraph. Some words will not be used.

foist	consternation	coterie	comprise
plethora	innocuous	eidetic	

1. Each month, a[n] _____ of radio-controlled model airplane enthu-siasts meets at an open field at the Ames farm, weather permitting (to the group's _____, rain has canceled two meetings this summer). The group _____ aviation fans from all over the county, and members with years of aeronautical experience offer a[n] _____ of knowledge and experience to amateurs in the club. The farmer who owns the field sees the meetings as _____, as long as no one crashes a plane into his house or his livestock.

From the list below, supply the words needed to complete the paragraph. Some words will not be used.

foist	vitriolic	innocuous	preamble
anomaly	flippancy	expiate	

2. Heather made a[n] _____ phone call when she realized that the crooked electronics shop had just _____ a cheap replica of a brand-name digital camera on her, but charged her the price of the genuine cam-era. No one answered the phone at the store, so Heather went, in person, to address her concern. When Heather entered the store, the owner con-fronted her. In his _____, he scolded Heather for her _____ in spreading such nasty, unfounded rumors about the business; then, quietly, so the other customers didn't hear, the owner offered to _____ his offense by offering Heather a more expensive camera at no additional cost. Heather simply shook her head and demanded her money back.

From the list below, supply the words needed to complete the paragraph. Some words will not be used.

anomaly	coterie	compendium	expiate
eidetic	incongruous	disconcert	

3.   Allen has a[n] _____ memory when it comes to remembering faces, so it was quite a[n] _____ when a stranger asked, "Don't you know me?" and Allen was forced to say "No." The stranger issued a simple, "You'll remember," before leaving Allen's store. The visit _____ Allen; he hated having a[n] _____ gap in the memory he often boasted about. That evening at home, Allen perused every _____ of customer names and addresses he could find, hoping to spark his memory.

EXERCISE II—Sentence Completion

Complete the sentence in a way that shows you understand the meaning of the italicized vocabulary word.

1. Ed could not get over his *consternation* when he saw…

2. In a *preamble* to the novel, the author writes…

3. The museum director has a *compendium* that categorizes…

4. That spider is *innocuous*, so…

5. Private Miller quickly departed from his usual *flippancy* when…

6. Ben saw that the theory *disconcerted* his students, so he…

7. The *anomaly* in the clouds turned out to be…

8. To gain membership in the *coterie* of artists, applicants had to…

9. The average dinner salad usually *comprises*…

10. On the street corner, a shady-looking man tried to *foist*…

11. Mike's fear at the sight of blood was *incongruous* with his…

12. Lyle received a *vitriolic* lecture from his teacher for…

13. Heidi could not *expiate* her crime, so she…

14. The old man forgot many things, but he still had an *eidetic* memory of the day he…

15. After a lengthy search, the starving castaways were thrilled to discover that the tiny island offered a *plethora* of…

EXERCISE III—Roots, Prefixes, and Suffixes

Study the entries and answer the questions that follow.

The root *ject* means "throw."
The root *tract* means "drag" or "draw."
The prefix *con* means "together."
The prefix *de* means "down."
The prefix *in* means "not."
The prefix *pro* means "forward."

1. *Using literal translations as guidance, define the following words without using a dictionary.*

   A. conjecture   D. injection
   B. dejected   E. detract
   C. intractable   F. protracted

2. What does a *projector* literally do?

3. When the prefix *ex*, which means "out," is added to the root *ject*, a letter drops out. What word do we get from this prefix and root?

4. Something that *draws* people *together* legally is a _____.

5. List as many words as you can think of that contain the root *ject*.

6. List as many words as you can think of that contain the prefix *con*.

EXERCISE IV—Inference

Complete the sentences by inferring information about the italicized word from its context.

1. If the editor's *vitriolic* critique of the novel brings the writer to tears, then the editor must think that...

2. A cheese merchant might have a *compendium* that lists...

3. If a doctor finds an *anomaly* on someone's X-ray, then the patient will probably want to...

EXERCISE V—Writing

Here is a writing prompt similar to the one you will find on the writing portion of the SAT.

Plan and write an essay based on the following statement:

"Rules and models destroy genius and art."
–William Hazlitt (1778-1830): *On Taste*

Assignment: For centuries, much debate has surrounded the question of "What is art?" Hazlitt's quote seems to suggest that rules and models destroy art; but without them, can art, as we know it, exist? In an essay, explain whether or not you agree with Hazlitt, and explain how you think art should be judged or determined. Support your opinion using evidence from your reading, studies, or experience and observations.

Thesis: Write a one-sentence response to the above assignment. Make certain this sentence offers a clear statement of your position.

Example: Rules and models do nothing but restrict new ways of thinking and stifle the endeavors of the next Einsteins and Michelangelos of the world.

Organizational Plan: If your thesis is the point on which you want to end, where does your essay need to begin? List the points of development that are inevitable in leading your reader from your beginning point to your end point. This list is your outline.

Draft: Use your thesis as both your beginning and your end. Following your outline, write a good first draft of your essay. Remember to support all of your points with examples, facts, references to reading, etc.

Review and revise: Exchange essays with a classmate. Using the scoring guide for Sentence Formation and Variety on page 250, score your partner's essay (while he or she scores yours). Focus on sentence structure and the use of language conventions. If necessary, rewrite your essay to improve the sentence structure and your use of language.

Identifying Sentence Errors

Identify the grammatical error in each of the following sentences. If the sentence contains no error, select answer E.

1. <u>Everyone in the office laughs</u> at Betty <u>because she felt she was</u> the
        (A)   (B)

    smartest person <u>who</u> <u>had ever worked</u> for the company. <u>No error</u>
                   (C)   (D)   (E)

2. The <u>man in the water shouted,</u> <u>"Help!"</u> when he <u>started to get tired from</u>
              (A)   (B)   (C)

    all the <u>swimming he done.</u>   <u>No error</u>
             (D)   (E)

3. If you dig <u>farther and deeper</u> into Bill's reason for embezzling the money
                 (A)

    from <u>his father's company,</u> you will see <u>that the crime began</u> when the
          (B)   (C)

    older man <u>removed him from the will.</u>   <u>No error</u>
              (D)   (E)

4. The <u>children all of who had all been playing noisily in their backyard fled</u>
                   (A)

    to the <u>safety of the back porch</u> at the <u>first sound of thunder,</u> which is
            (B)   (C)

    exactly what <u>their parents had told them to do.</u> <u>No error</u>
               (D)   (E)

5. <u>No one</u> in the entire class <u>could understand exactly</u> what the teacher
      (A)   (B)

    <u>meant when she</u> talked about oxygen and <u>it's properties.</u> <u>No error</u>
      (C)   (D)   (E)

Improving Sentences

The underlined portion of each sentence below contains some flaw. Select the answer that best corrects the flaw.

6. The young girl <u>wanted to go to see whoever her parents wanted to see, and whenever they wanted to go.</u>
    A. wanted to see whoever her parents wanted, and whenever they wanted to go.
    B. wanted to see whomever her parents wanted to see, and whenever they wanted to see them.
    C. wanted to visit whomever her parents wanted whenever they wanted to go.
    D. wanted to go to see whomever her parents wanted to see, and whenever the parents wanted to go.
    E. wanted to go to see whoever her parents wanted to see, whenever they wanted to.

7. <u>The butterflies, which emerged from their cocoons this year, will</u> not be the same ones that migrate to Mexico for the winter.
    A. The butterflies, that emerged from their cocoons this year, will
    B. The butterflies, which climbed out of their cocoons this year, will
    C. Every butterfly, which emerged from its cocoons this year, will
    D. The butterflies that emerged from their cocoons this year will
    E. Whichever butterflies that have emerged from their cocoons this year will

8. <u>Everybody involved in the student plays last Saturday and Sunday are to receive</u> an extra day to study before finals.
    A. Everyone involved in the student plays last Saturday and Sunday are to receive
    B. Everybody involved in the student plays last Saturday and Sunday is to receive
    C. Everybody involved in the student plays last Saturday and Sunday will have received
    D. Everybody in the student plays last Saturday and Sunday are to receive
    E. Everybody involved in last Saturday's and Sunday's student plays are to receive

9. Playing in the park, the stormy weather ruined the childrens' game of dodge ball.
    A. The stormy weather ruined the childrens' game of dodge ball playing in the park.
    B. The stormy weather ruined the childrens' game of dodge ball.
    C. Playing in the park, the stormy weather ruined the children's game of dodge ball.
    D. The stormy weather ruined the childrens' game of dodge ball who were playing in the park.
    E. The stormy weather ruined the children's dodge ball game in the park.

10. Anyone who comes to the football game wearing a player's T-shirt receive 50% off the price of admission.
    A. Anyone, who comes to the football game wearing a player's T-shirt, will receive
    B. Everybody who come to the football game wearing a player's T-shirt will receive
    C. Anyone who comes to the football game wearing a player's T-shirt receives
    D. Anyone who comes to the game wearing a T-shirt will receive
    E. Anyone who comes to the football game, and also who wears a player's T-shirt shall receive

Lesson Six

1. **sectarian** (sek târ´ ē ən) *adj.* narrowly confined to a particular group
   Members of the *sectarian* cult gave no thought to the beliefs of outsiders.
   syn: insular; dogmatic   *ant: tolerant*

2. **peregrination** (per i grə nāt´ shən) *n.* travel by walking
   Vince planned a summer of *peregrination* throughout Europe.
   syn: trekking; exploration

3. **accoutrement** (ə kōō´ trə mənt) *n.* an accessory item of dress or
       equipment
   Various *accoutrements* dangled from the workbelt of the telephone
   repairman.
   syn: device; gear

4. **contrive** (kən trīv´) *v.* to plan cleverly; to devise
   After four days in captivity, Steve *contrived* an escape plan that could not
   fail.
   syn: concoct; design; engineer

5. **hubris** (hyōō´ bris) *n.* overbearing pride; arrogance
   Hubris is the character flaw found in many tragic heroes.
   syn: conceit; smugness; pompousness   *ant: humility; modesty*

6. **platitude** (plat´ i tōōd) *n.* an obvious remark; a cliché
   The two candidates offered plenty of *platitudes*, but no practical
   solutions.
   syn: banality; maxim; truism

7. **venerate** (ven´ ə rāt) *v.* to respect or revere
   Young scholars often *venerate* the ideas of the great philosophers.
   syn: glorify; treasure   *ant: abhor; despise*

8. **scullion** (skul´ yən) *n.* a servant for menial tasks
   Scullions scrubbed the castle floors for hours prior to the king's feast.
   syn: peon; toiler   *ant: patrician; aristocrat*

9. **quotidian** (kwō ti´ dē ən) *adj.* everyday; commonplace
   Earthquakes were *quotidian* events for the people living near the volcano.
   syn: ordinary; routine   *ant: rare; uncommon*

10. **prognosticate** (präg näs´ tə kāt) v. to predict
    Meteorologists are attempting to *prognosticate* the path of the hurricane.
    syn: forecast; foreshadow

11. **antediluvian** (an ti də lōō´ vē ən) *adj.* extremely old; antiquated
    Especially tall structures were rare in the ancient world because
    antediluvian architecture could not withstand the enormous forces.
    syn: ancient; archaic   *ant: modern; new*

12. **stringent** (strin´ jənt) *adj.* restrictive; imposing demanding standards
    The dynamite factory imposed *stringent* safety rules to prevent any
    catastrophe.
    syn: severe; rigid; inflexible   *ant: lenient; flexible*

13. **haughty** (hô´ tē) *adj.* condescendingly proud; arrogant
    The *haughty* boy thought that his family's wealth made him better than
    other students.
    syn: conceited; snobbish; supercilious   *ant: humble; modest*

14. **sanctimonious** (sangk tə mō´ nə əs) *adj.* showing false piety or
        righteousness
    The *sanctimonious* landlord made public contributions to charities, but
    threatened his tenants with eviction if they didn't pay the rent on time.
    syn: hypocritical; specious   *ant: humble; modest*

15. **imbroglio** (im brōl´ yō) *n.* a difficult and embarrassing situation
    His infatuation with a married co-worker led to an *imbroglio* at the office
    picnic.
    syn: predicament   *ant: peace; serenity*

EXERCISE I—Words in Context

From the list below, supply the words needed to complete the paragraph. Some words will not be used.

imbroglio	quotidian	sanctimonious	scullion
peregrination	hubris	prognosticate	

1.   There was a[n] _____ at the garage. A customer arrived and demanded to see his car, after having been told that the repairs were nearly finished, but found that the work had not even begun.

"Two weeks ago, you _____ that the job would take three or four days," the customer said to Jane, the receptionist. "Give me the keys; I'll take my car to a different garage." Jane complied, still smiling as usual; she never worried about losing an occasional customer, though she did feel bad about mistakenly telling the customer that his car was finished. Angry customers were a[n] _____ occurrence in the auto repair business; most people have a tendency to become emotional when they receive bills for hundreds or even thousands of dollars, especially for repairs to cars that are still relatively new. Unlike the angry customer, Jane knew that every garage in town was overloaded. Upon hearing the customer's story, the other garage would offer some _____ criticism of Jane's garage, accept the job, and then do exactly what Jane's garage did, since the car required a tedious repair that yielded little profit. The whole frustrating process simply causes many drivers to abandon their cars and resort to _____ as their primary form of transportation.

From the list below, supply the words needed to complete the paragraph. Some words will not be used.

platitude	haughty	contrive	stringent
sectarian	quotidian	scullions	

2.   After reviewing the pamphlets for the private school, Veronica's parents thought that the school might be too _____ because of its religious affiliation, but they favored the _____ educational requirements to which the students were held.

Veronica assumed that the private school would be full of _____, rich children who probably treated middle-class people like _____. She was about to _____ a way to get out of going to the school, but at the last minute she decided to give it a try.

From the list below, supply the words needed to complete the paragraph. Some words will not be used.

accoutrement	hubris	platitude	prognosticate
venerate	antediluvian	contrive	

3.   Most people rendered a typical _____ to Tracey before the triathlon, such as "Good luck," or "Pace yourself," but Tracey's mother, who _____ historical matriarchs and _____ conquerors such as Cleopatra, simply said, "Win the race or don't bother starting it." Tracey smiled as she removed her watch, earrings, and other _____ before walking to the triathlon's registration booth. Tracey also hoped that her own _____ hadn't clouded her own expectations of how well she would do in the race; she was in excellent shape, but so were the other two hundred competitors.

EXERCISE II—Sentence Completion

Complete the sentence in a way that shows you understand the meaning of the italicized vocabulary word.

1.   The thief found himself in an *imbroglio* when he...

2.   Our *sectarian* neighbors seldom speak to us because they...

3.   The corrupt police commissioner often made the *sanctimonious* claim that he...

4.   *Peregrination* was the most common form of transportation before...

5.   Kevin left the country club because he didn't like the way in which *haughty* members...

6.   Ashley bought the new dress, but she still needed *accoutrements* such as...

7.   Carol, the secretary, began to feel like the boss's *scullion* when he told her to...

8.   Cindy *venerates* the huge walnut tree on the property line, but Bill, her neighbor, would like to...

9.   Rachel warned her son that his *hubris*, left unchecked, would...

10. Nathan was tired of watching *quotidian* television sitcoms, so he…

11. Rabbits and woodchucks were eating the vegetables in the garden, so Bob *contrived* a way to…

12. Noticing the sudden drop in temperature and the dark clouds on the horizon, the ship's captain *prognosticated* that…

13. Watching a movie with our father is difficult because he feels obligated to voice some *platitude* every time…

14. Dana was certain that she could meet the *stringent* training requirements of…

15. People of the remote mountain village retained *antediluvian* traditions that…

EXERCISE III—Roots, Prefixes, and Suffixes

Study the entries and answer the questions that follow.

The prefix *pre* means "before."
The root *bene* means "good" or "well."
The root *optim* means "best."
The root *dict* means "speech."
The root *ven* means "come."
The prefix *contra* means "against."
The prefix *con* means "together."

1. *Using literal translations as guidance, define the following words without using a dictionary.*

    A. contradiction   D. optimal
    B. optimistic   E. contravene
    C. convene   F. benediction

2. The root *male* has the opposite meaning of the root *bene*. What, then, is a *malediction*?

3. What do you suppose a *venue* is?

4. If you *talk* about something *before* it happens, then you might be making a[n] _____.

5. List as many words as you can think of that contain the root *dict*.

6. List as many words as you can think of that contain the root *bene*.

EXERCISE IV—Inference

Complete the sentences by inferring information about the italicized word from its context.

1. A university might have *stringent* academic requirements for admission to ensure that...

2. During a *quotidian* visit to the grocery store, you probably wouldn't expect to...

3. Devoted fans might *venerate* their idol long after...

EXERCISE V—Critical Reading

Below is a reading passage followed by several multiple-choice questions similar to the ones you will encounter on the SAT. Carefully read the passage and choose the best answer to each of the questions.

The following passage describes the characteristics of the Maya, Inca, and Aztec cultures of Central and South America.

To many, the mere mention of Mayan, Aztec, or Incan civilization evokes thoughts of great, flat-topped pyramids of mysterious origin, secret cities perched on remote mountaintops, and booby-trapped temples brimming with treasure-hoards of gold. Indeed, impressions have not changed much since the age of the
5　Spanish explorers, who, despite intentions of conquest, were also mystified by the cryptic civilizations of Mesoamerica and South America. Explorers may not have found the mythical golden city of El Dorado, but they did find three amazing cultures, each with unique characteristics.

Mayan civilization, often considered to be the most exalted and mysterious of
10　the three, inhabited the Yucatan Peninsula of Eastern Mexico as long ago as 2600 B.C. Emerging from a collection of city-states with no central government, the Maya reached a cultural peak between A.D. 250 and 900. The Maya, who developed an astrological calendar that allowed them to grow crops in poor soil, were

originally thought to be a peaceful people, but archaeologists have since deter-
15   mined that intertribal warfare brought about their decline. Mayans, like the Aztecs
and Incas, also practiced human sacrifice. Ancient pyramids inscribed with weathered glyphs and characters from the most advanced ancient alphabet in the
western hemisphere now sit abandoned, obscured by centuries of jungle growth.
Mayan descendents still inhabit the Yucatan, but the technology, religion, and prac-
20   tices of the ancient civilization must now be slowly exhumed and catalogued by
archaeologists.

The Aztecs, noted perhaps most often for their penchant for battle and human
sacrifice, composed the second-largest pre-Columbian civilization in South
America. Originally a nomadic society inhabiting the central basin of Mexico, the
25   various tribes who identified themselves as Aztec settled in the marshy region near
Lake Texcoco and, in 1325, founded the city of Tenochtitlan at the present site of
Mexico City. Despite vicious religious practices, the Aztec demonstrated ingenuity
by inventing an innovative farming technique to grow crops among the 30 canals
of Tenochtitlan. Farmers built chinampas, or artificial, fertile islands floating in
30   canals, to grow crops of beans, peppers, avocados, tomatoes, and, most important,
corn. Ironically, the seemingly bloodthirsty culture, when not participating in an
estimated 20,000 human sacrifices a year, took great interest in the beauty of
nature; Aztecs, who lacked plows or beasts of burden, took the time to grow beautiful flowers strictly for decoration. Before falling to the Spanish in 1521, the
35   Aztecs left several permanent contributions to history and to the explorers of the
New World: chocolate, derived from indigenous cacao beans; tomatoes, potatoes,
and numerous other vegetables that have long become staples to the rest of the
world; and, as testament to the artisans among the Aztecs, an accurate, 24-ton
limestone calendar that took more than fifty years to construct.
40   Incas, whose feats of engineering baffle modern architects, dominated the west
coast of South America from 1300 to 1535. Like the Aztecs, the Incas practiced
human sacrifice and lacked a written language; however, the Incas made up for
language shortcomings with advanced architecture and a complex government. In
addition to having the most advanced medical and surgical techniques of the
45   ancient Americas, the Incas constructed more than 12,000 miles of roadway and
aqueducts to supply taxpaying and labor-contributing tribes throughout the
empire. The precise, intricate stonemasonry of Incan pyramids, fortresses, and
walls commands the respect of even modern masons. Incan architecture still dots
the Andean mountains and highlands as the timeless endeavors of a lost people.
50   So despite the achievements and predominance of the two civilizations intact
after Columbus arrived in the New World, they found themselves at the mercy of
the Spaniards during the sixteenth century. Hernando Cortez, who sought control
of the Aztec Empire, or Mexican Empire, began his quest in 1519 by forming
alliances with tribes who were displeased with the leadership of Montezuma II in
55   Tenochtitlan. Cortez went to the city and took Montezuma hostage, taking advantage of the fact that Aztecs thought that the Spaniards were descendents of their
god, Quetzalcoatl, and had come to fulfill a prophecy. Montezuma was killed during a short uprising in 1521 while instructing the Aztecs to make peace with the
Spaniards. The Spaniards were forced to retreat from the city, but they soon
60   regrouped and besieged the Aztec capital. After the eventual surrender, Cortez
burned the city and destroyed the greatest monuments of Aztec culture.

The Incan Empire shared a fate similar to that of the Aztec, but at the hands of a conquistador more sinister than Cortez. Francisco Pizarro, motivated by legends of treasure, captured the Incan ruler Atahualpa during their first meeting.
65 Atahualpa offered a ransom for himself that consisted of a roomful of gold. Atahualpa revealed the location of the treasure to Pizarro, and Pizarro promptly executed the ruler and seized control of Cuzco, the Incan capital. Pizarro was eventually killed by his own people, but the Incan Empire was forever lost.

Aztecs, Incas, and Mayans who escaped the iron swords and gunpowder of the
70 Europeans instead suffered the old world diseases that accompanied the explorers. Entire tribes vanished as smallpox, scarlet fever, and influenza decimated the native population of the Americas. Those who survived were forced to abandon their customs and live beneath Spanish rule for the next three centuries.

Millions of tourists now visit Mexico and Peru to see the remnants of the Mayan,
75 Aztec, and Inca civilizations. Though weathered or overgrown, the relics stand as permanent markers of the ingenuity and art of the pre-Columbian civilizations. Archaeologists and treasure hunters scour newly discovered burial platforms and caves in search of knowledge that might contribute to the modern understanding of the lost cultures, and also, undoubtedly, to find relics made of that one material
80 valued by both the ancient and modern worlds: gold.

1. The purpose of this passage is to
   A. explain how Spanish explorers decimated other cultures.
   B. demonstrate the differences among three early cultures.
   C. show early cultural advances.
   D. show the relationships among the three cultures.
   E. explain how three civilizations began.

2. The term *Mesoamerica* most nearly means
   A. South America.
   B. coastal America.
   C. prehistoric America.
   D. ancient America.
   E. Middle America.

3. It is ironic that the Aztecs grew flowers because
   A. flowers do not grow well where the Aztecs lived.
   B. flower nurseries are indicative of a society with leisure time.
   C. the Aztecs were violent and warlike.
   D. Aztecs had no calendar to determine the best time to grow flowers.
   E. pre-Columbian cultures did not use plants for decorations.

4. The term *pre-Columbian* describes
   A. all civilization that preceded the nation of Columbia.
   B. the time leading to the foundation of Washington, D.C.
   C. everything before the year in which the Inca Empire fell.
   D. the new name that Cortez gave to Tenochtitlan.
   E. the time before Columbus arrived in the Americas in 1492.

5. The word *staple* most nearly means
   A. to fasten.
   B. a basic dietary item.
   C. a luxurious food.
   D. a feature.
   E. an overabundance.

6. Which of the following statements is implied by the following quotation (lines 45-47)?

   > "...the Incas constructed more than 12,000 miles of roadway and aqueducts to supply taxpaying...tribes throughout the empire."

   A. The Incas had some type of central government.
   B. Incan roadways were elevated high above the ground.
   C. High taxes probably accelerated the fall of the Incan Empire.
   D. Incas wasted resources on building roadways.
   E. Incas decorated their aqueducts with gold.

7. Unlike the Aztecs and Incas, the Mayans had
   A. knowledge of planting crops.
   B. a written language.
   C. human sacrifice.
   D. chinampas.
   E. a calendar.

8. The passage contains no details about the Spanish conquering the Mayans because
   A. the Mayans welcomed the Spaniards.
   B. all Mayan people mysteriously disappeared in A.D. 1450.
   C. the Portuguese conquered the Mayans, and this passage focuses on the Spanish.
   D. Mayan civilization declined before the Europeans arrived.
   E. Europe had no interests in the Yucatan peninsula.

9. Which choice would be the best title for this passage?
    A. Differentiating Ancient Cultures
    B. Human Sacrifice in Three Civilizations
    C. Aztec, Inca, and Maya, in South America
    D. Three Lost Civilizations
    E. The History of Ancient Mexico and Parts of South America

10. The author of this passage would probably agree that
    A. explorers should not have interfered with the Mesoamerican or South American cultures.
    B. human sacrifice is an acceptable practice.
    C. the Aztecs were far more advanced than the Incas.
    D. gold is more important than information about the civilizations.
    E. the Spaniards were devious in the way they conquered the Aztecs and Incas.

Lesson Seven

1. **gibberish** (jib´ ər ish) *n.* nonsense; unintelligible speech
   A foreign language might sound like *gibberish* until you learn key words and phrases.
   syn: babble; chatter; prattle

2. **inimical** (i nim´ i kəl) *adj.* unfriendly; hostile; injurious
   The stranger's *inimical* voice made me wonder if I had done something wrong.
   syn: mean; malicious; harmful   *ant: encouraging; flattering*

3. **nexus** (nek´ səs) *n.* a link, tie, or bond
   The desire for acceptance by others is a *nexus* for all humankind.
   syn: connection; correlation   *ant: disruption; gap*

4. **coeval** (kō ē´ vəl) *adj.* of the same time period
   Scientists assert that the two ancient, *coeval* civilizations, though thousands of miles apart, were aware of each other.
   syn: contemporaneous

5. **dilatory** (di´ lə tōr ē) *adj.* tending to delay or procrastinate
   The teacher warned the *dilatory* students that any paper turned in after the deadline would be an instant failure.
   syn: dallying; laggard; unhurried   *ant: diligent; prompt*

6. **convoluted** (kon´ və lōōt əd) *adj.* complicated; intricate
   Few people in class understood the teacher's *convoluted* explanation of the problem.
   syn: involved; jumbled   *ant: simple; obvious*

7. **entreat** (en trēt´) *v.* to earnestly request or petition
   At the supermarket, the child first *entreated* his mother for the candy bar, and then cried for it.
   syn: importune; implore   *ant: demand*

8. **anecdote** (an´ ik dōt) *n.* a short account of an incident
   New parents often share *anecdotes* about their children.
   syn: narrative

9. **incumbent** (in kum´ bənt) *adj.* obligatory; necessary
   It is *incumbent* on the night watchman to stay awake during his shift.
   syn: required; essential   *ant: voluntary; unnecessary*

10. **churlish** (chûr´ lish) *adj.* boorish or vulgar
    The wild cowboys' *churlish* behavior offended the genteel townspeople.
    syn: uncouth; rude; surly   *ant: courteous; polished; civil*

11. **promulgate** (prom´ əl gāt) *v.* to announce; to make known
    During the drought, the city *promulgated* strict rules about water usage.
    syn: declare; exhibit

12. **staid** (stād) *adj.* showing dignity and often strait-laced propriety
    The *staid* general spoke softly, seldom dismounted his horse, and never smiled.
    syn: composed; serious; solemn   *ant: agitated; excited; nervous*

13. **livid** (liv´ id) *adj.* extremely angry
    When I was brought home by the police, my father was *livid*; he yelled at me for hours.
    syn: enraged; furious; fuming   *ant: contented; pleased*

14. **lurid** (lŏŏr´ id) *adj.* shocking; explicit
    The *lurid* crime appeared in every newspaper in the city.
    syn: sensational; extreme   *ant: dull; boring; mediocre*

15. **cogent** (kō´ jənt) *adj.* convincing; reasonable
    Bert's *cogent* justification for a new desk convinced management to buy one for him.
    syn: compelling; pertinent; influential   *ant: ineffective; weak*

EXERCISE I—Words in Context

From the list below, supply the words needed to complete the paragraph. Some words will not be used.

gibberish	**livid**	**staid**	**promulgate**
cogent	**incumbent**	**nexus**	

1. The boss was _____ after he learned about the accounting error that cost the company thousands of dollars, but he vowed to remain _____ while he sought a[n] _____ explanation for the mistake. This was the second major error in six months, and it was _____ on the company to find the source of the problem. When confronted, the nervous accountant quickly listed possible excuses for what might have gone wrong.

    "Spare me your _____ and tell me exactly where the error originated," ordered the boss.

From the list below, supply the words needed to complete the paragraph. Some words will not be used.

lurid	**cogent**	**anecdote**	**entreat**
inimical	**nexus**	**coeval**	

2. When the children asked their father about an old, abandoned cabin in the forest behind their house, he responded with a[n] _____ about the day he discovered it, when he, too, was eleven years old.

    "Enos, a[n] _____ hermit, once lived in that shack," said father, "and he used to shoot at anyone who dared to trespass on his property. The old man, rumored to be an escaped convict hiding from the law, was the last member of a family _____ with the bootlegging industry that flourished in these woods during the Prohibition Era."

    The _____ story so fascinated the children that they had to venture into the forest to look at the rotting timbers of the overgrown cabin once again. The father's memory was now a[n] _____ that connected the children's generation to a lost era, and the children planned to access that link more often in the future.

From the list below, supply the words needed to complete the paragraph. Some words will not be used.

dilatory	convoluted	entreat	gibberish
churlish	promulgate	nexus	

3.   Roger _____ his teacher for more time, but she told him to put his pencil down and hand in his test like everyone else. Once again, Roger's _____ approach to test-taking had resulted in another incomplete exam, but he blamed it on the _____ word problems on which he had spent too much time. He stood and _____ to the rest of the class his obvious failure by making the whistling sound of a bomb falling from the sky and then exploding on the ground. The teacher then asked Roger to take his _____ behavior outside.

EXERCISE II—Sentence Completion

Complete the sentence in a way that shows you understand the meaning of the italicized vocabulary word.

1. Craig was *livid* after learning that…

2. Maggie failed to give Sam a *cogent* reason for…

3. Aaron could speak only *gibberish* after having his wisdom teeth removed because…

4. Dave *entreated* his messy roommate to…

5. The athlete remained *staid* despite…

6. The *lurid* crime of Irene's next-door neighbor…

7. Getting an occasional checkup is *incumbent* on anyone who…

8. The detective's voice had an *inimical* tone when he…

9. At the class reunion, alumni shared *anecdotes* about…

10. Dinosaurs were not *coeval* with humankind, so early humans did not need to…

11. When the teacher saw the *churlish* message on Gary's tee shirt, she told him to…

12. Shawn knew that his *dilatory* work habits would…

13. The movie stars did not *promulgate* their engagement because…

14. The teacher asked the student to revise the *convoluted* essay so that…

15. A song that never seems to fade in popularity is sometimes called a generational *nexus* because…

EXERCISE III—Roots, Prefixes, and Suffixes

Study the entries and answer the questions that follow.

The root *spect* means "look."
The roots *vid* and *vis* mean "see."
The root *aud* means "hear."
The prefix *circum* means "around."
The prefix *in* can mean "not," "upon," or "against."

1. Without using a dictionary, define the following words.

   A. auditory   D. spectator
   B. circumspect   E. invidious
   C. inaudible   F. spectrum

2. A place specifically designed for *hearing* music, speeches, or recitals, is called a[n] _____.

3. What do you suppose a *specter* is?

4. List as many words as you can think of that contain the root *spect*.

5. List as many words as you can think of that contain the root *vis*.

EXERCISE IV—Inference

Complete the sentences by inferring information about the italicized word from its context.

1. If you miss an important exam, you might *entreat* the teacher to...

2. Someone who gives you an *inimical* stare might...

3. It was *incumbent* on the team to be successful because...

EXERCISE V—Writing

Here is a writing prompt similar to the one you will find on the writing portion of the SAT.

Plan and write an essay on the following statement:

> In the ordinary course of nature, the great beneficent changes come slowly and silently. The noisy changes, for the most part, mean violence and disruption. The roar of storms and tornadoes, the explosions of volcanoes, the crash of thunder, are the result of a sudden break in the equipoise of the elements; from a condition of comparative repose and silence they become fearfully swift and audible. The still small voice is the voice of life and growth and perpetuity. In the history of a nation, it is the same.
>
> –John Burroughs (1832-1921)

Assignment: In an essay, explain whether Burroughs is accurate in his comparison of nature with civilization. Cite an example or examples from American history that best illustrate Burroughs' comparison. Support your position by discussing examples from literature, art, history, or experience or observation.

Thesis: Write a one-sentence response to the above assignment. Make certain this sentence offers a clear statement of your position.

Example: Burroughs is indeed correct that mankind follows the same pattern as that of the natural world, and this parallelism is quite visible in the United States Civil War.

Organizational Plan: If your thesis is the point on which you want to end, where does your essay need to begin? List the points of development that are inevitable in leading your reader from your beginning point to your end point. This list is your outline.

Draft: Use your thesis as both your beginning and your end. Following your outline, write a good first draft of your essay. Remember to support all of your points with examples, facts, references to reading, etc.

Review and revise: Exchange essays with a classmate. Using the scoring guide for Word Choice on page 251, score your partner's essay (while he or she scores yours). Focus on word choice and the use of language conventions. If necessary, rewrite your essay to improve the word choice and use of language.

Improving Paragraphs

Read the following passage and then answer the multiple-choice questions that follow. The questions will require you to make decisions regarding the revision of the reading selection.

(1) Have you ever driven down the road, seemingly at ease, perhaps exceeding the speed limit to arrive at your destination a bit more quickly. (2) Then you see a long line of cars waiting in line to pay the toll and realize that you now have to join them and become one of the poor idiots wasting time and costly gasoline. (3) People have engaged in this meaningless exercise ever since toll roads and toll bridges were invented. (4) Stop, go a few feet, brake, stop again, and then repeat the process more times than you can count as cars jostle for better positions like basketball players near the hoop. (5) Drivers nervously dig in ashtrays and between car seats, fumbling for the correct change, dropping coins on the ground or attempting to back up, or their cars scrape the side of the tollbooth, leaving paint chips and chipped concrete as permanent marks of futility. (6) Sometimes you're in line for ten minutes or more before you reach the toll-taker and surrender your quarter, dollar, or life savings for the privilege of being on a supposedly fast route home.

(7) Modern technology has finally given drivers the means of escaping the horrors of paying tolls by hand. (8) New microchip transmitters affixed to windshields can be read by machines above the tollbooths, and the charges are billed automatically to drivers' credit cards. (9) This easy process requires drivers to register their cars, set up accounts, and pay the bill, that's all there is to it, it's as simple as that. (10) The driver can pass through the toll lane without stopping, while the fools in the pay-by-cash lane wait their turns.

(11) The rewards of using the simple, plastic stick-ons are enormous: drivers save time and gas; some states offer discounts to those who use the devices; pollution decreases; fewer accidents occur; and there's no worrying about having enough cash for the toll.

(12) Few things in life compare to the thrill of watching other drivers suffer the wrenching pain of losing time waiting in long lines—even such joys as graduation, finding money on the ground, getting a bike for Christmas, and falling in love. (13) It is this great pleasure in observing someone elses misfortune that separates us from the animals—not our ability to reason or use tools. (14) Humans love to gloat! (15) My own toll transmitter will arrive in the mail next week, and I'll then be able to enjoy the pleasure of smoothly gliding through booth after booth without having to stop.

(16) So, if you're in the long line waiting to move an inch at a time for an hour because you're not intelligent enough to join the modern world, wave to me as I glide on by, because I'll be looking over at you with a smile on my face and a transmitter on my windshield.

(17) Some paranoid people think this new use of electronic gadgetry is just another diabolical invention of the government for tracking citizens, so that it knows where we are, where we go, what we buy, and what we do. (18) That form of reasoning is illogical and false. (19) If the government wants to follow people's

whereabouts, there are already plenty of ways to do so, like security cameras, Internet data gathering, bank reports, passport information, credit card statements, social security numbers, taxes, cell phone monitoring, etc. (20) One more intrusion into our personal lives will not make any difference at all. (21) To those people who refuse to get these electronic passes, I say, "If you don't have anything to hide, why worry?"

1. Which choice best corrects an error in paragraph 1?
   A. Find a substitute for the word *idiots*.
   B. Delete sentence 4.
   C. Exchange sentence 2 and sentence 5.
   D. End the first sentence with a question mark.
   E. Rewrite the first paragraph from the first-person point of view.

2. To correct an error in paragraph 2, an editor would need to
   A. create two sentences from sentence 7.
   B. place a semicolon between sentence 7 and sentence 8.
   C. fix the comma splices in sentence 9.
   D. move sentence 9 to the beginning of the paragraph.
   E. explain the layout of the toll lane mentioned in sentence 10.

3. Which choice corrects a grammatical error in sentence 13?
   A. Replace *us* with *them*.
   B. Replace *elses* with *else's*.
   C. Create an antecedent for *else*.
   D. Remove the comma splice.
   E. Make *use tools* parallel with *to reason*.

4. Which of the following revisions would improve the chronology of the passage?
   A. Exchange paragraphs 1 and 2.
   B. Exchange paragraphs 2 and 3.
   C. Exchange paragraphs 3 and 4.
   D. Exchange paragraphs 5 and 6.
   E. Exchange paragraphs 1 and 6.

5. If one paragraph must be removed from the passage, the best choice would be
   A. paragraph 1, because an introduction is not necessary.
   B. paragraph 2, because an introduction to the microchip transmitters is not necessary.
   C. paragraph 3, because it does not support the topic of the passage.
   D. paragraph 4, because it digresses into personal philosophy.
   E. paragraph 6, because it challenges the topic of the passage.

REVIEW

Lessons 1 – 7

EXERCISE I – Sentence Completion

Choose the best pair of words to complete the sentence. Most choices will fit grammatically and will even make sense logically, but you must choose the pair that best fits the idea of the sentence.

Note that these words are not taken directly from lessons in this book. This exercise is intended to replicate the sentence completion portion of the SAT.

1. The action hero's behavior in the movie seemed _____ for the danger he was in; he sat _____ and waited for the bomb to explode, instead of breaking out of his chains and conquering the villains.
   A. inappropriate, dejectedly
   B. perfect, fearfully
   C. awful, ridiculously
   D. right, inertly
   E. inexplicable, smilingly

2. The magician practiced and practiced; she was trying to be _____, since the new trick required her to loosen the chains with her _____ hand.
   A. flexible, other
   B. powerful, muscular
   C. ambidextrous, unencumbered
   D. surreptitious, concealed
   E. nimble, left

3. The sirens sounded their _____ to warn people of the _____ air-raid drill.
   A. alarms, impending
   B. noises, close-by
   C. screeches, upcoming
   D. warnings, planned
   E. panic, necessary

4. Although he was a[n] _____ practical joker, nearly everyone who
    met Bill for the first time felt the man's warmth and _____.
    A. incorrigible, amiability
    B. ridiculous, humor
    C. incessant, respectability
    D. terrible, sensitivity
    E. incorruptible, temerity

5. The architect had _____ plans for the courthouse, but the
    _____ budget forced him to scale them back.
    A. conceived, unlimited
    B. completed, city's
    C. grandiose, minuscule
    D. major, weakened
    E. unfinished, ample

6. No peasant was allowed to approach the cruel emperor without showing
    the proper _____; anyone who did so was _____ executed.
    A. humility, rapidly
    B. obedience, consequently
    C. bowing, soon
    D. respectfulness, usually
    E. tradition, instantly

7. The theory that the Earth is flat was _____ disproved by Columbus'
    _____ voyage to the New World.
    A. simultaneously, second
    B. finally, record-breaking
    C. absolutely, dangerous
    D. conclusively, unprecedented
    E. accurately, ships'

8. He _____ the walls of his office with _____ of his advanced
    degrees because the original ones had been destroyed in a fire.
    A. filled, pictures
    B. lined, artifacts
    C. adorned, facsimiles
    D. created, copies
    E. decorated, blow-ups

EXERCISE II – Crossword Puzzle

Use the clues to complete the crossword puzzle. The answers consist of vocabulary words from lessons 1 through 7.

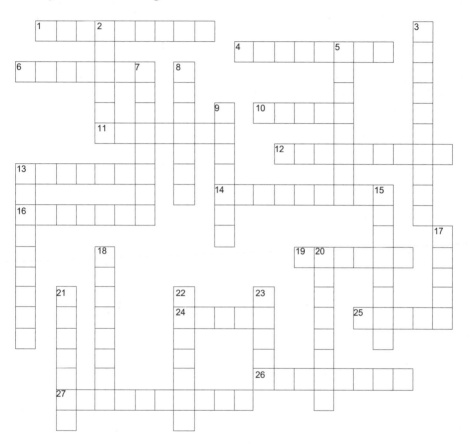

Across
1. release of emotional tension
4. clear
6. laughable
10. pass off as genuine
11. submissive
12. to waver
13. dark and forbidding
14. obligatory
16. full
19. dull recital
24. link
25. showing dignity
26. an overabundance
27. indifferent

Down
2. overbearing pride
3. occurring everywhere
5. plan cleverly
7. alienate
8. make amends for
9. trace of something
13. restrictive
15. shorten
17. shocking
18. servant
20. evil act
21. robber
22. odd occurrence
23. seize power

Lesson Eight

1. **pander** (pan´ dər) *v.* to exploit weaknesses of others; to cater to the
   vices of others
   The trendy clothing store *pandered* to materialistic clients by selling
   shoddy clothing at outrageously high prices.
   syn: cajole; indulge

2. **otiose** (ō´ shē ōs) *adj.* useless; futile
   The director decided to remove the *otiose* scenes that increased the
   length of the film but failed to add to the suspense.
   syn: unimportant; worthless   *ant: productive; necessary*

3. **puerile** (pyu´ ər əl) *adj.* childish; juvenile
   Uncle Joe refused to tolerate his teenage nephew's *puerile* behavior.
   syn: immature; infantile   *ant: mature*

4. **aleatory** (ā´ lē ə tôr ē) *adj.* dependent on luck or chance
   Because of the uncertain weather forecast, the success of our company
   picnic is purely *aleatory.*

5. **asperity** (a sper´ i tē) *n.* roughness or harshness; severity
   The teacher felt bad after his *asperity* caused a student to cry.
   syn: acerbity; irascibility   *ant: mildness; kindness*

6. **renunciation** (ri nun sē ā´ shən) *n.* rejection; refusal to acknowledge
   Members of the club responded to Bill's *renunciation* of their doctrine by
   asking him to leave.
   syn: denial; refusal   *ant: admittance; concession*

7. **unimpeachable** (un im pē´ chə bəl) *adj.* unquestionable; beyond
   doubt
   The Internet is not an *unimpeachable* source of information for academic
   research.
   syn: trustworthy; infallible   *ant: questionable; flawed*

8. **inveigh** (in vā´) *v.* to disapprove angrily; to protest
   Irene *inveighed* against her company's hiring of a former competitor for a
   prominent position.
   syn: berate; condemn; remonstrate   *ant: commend; laud; praise*

9. **lionize** (lī´ ə nīz) *v.* to assign great social importance to; to treat as a celebrity
The public *lionized* the boy for saving the child from the burning building.
syn: acclaim; exalt; honor   *ant: ignore; overlook*

10. **allay** (ə lā´) *v.* to relieve; to alleviate
Mom tried to *allay* my fear of flying by reading favorable airline statistics.
syn: calm; ease; pacify   *ant: excite; intensify; agitate*

11. **vitiate** (vish´ ē āt) *v.* to corrupt morally; to contaminate
Mark claims that prisons simply *vitiate* the spirits of the inmates.
syn: defile; devalue; spoil   *ant: purify; clarify; cleanse*

12. **recalcitrant** (ri kal´ si trənt) *adj.* stubbornly resistant; showing opposition
The *recalcitrant* child kicked and screamed when the barber tried to give him his first haircut.
syn: defiant; insubordinate; unwilling   *ant: agreeable; obedient*

13. **exegesis** (ek sə jē´ sis) *n.* an explanation of a text; a critical interpretation
The students read an *exegesis* of *Macbeth* to understand the play better.
syn: analysis; exposition; commentary

14. **ameliorate** (ə mēl´ yə rāt) *v.* to make better; to improve
The manager asked for suggestions that might *ameliorate* working conditions at the factory.
syn: enhance; upgrade   *ant: weaken; damage; corrupt*

15. **profligate** (prof´ li git) *adj.* wasteful and immoral
The young heir lived a *profligate* life of alcohol, excess, and greed.
syn: licentious; decadent   *ant: virtuous; principled*

EXERCISE I—Words in Context

From the list below, supply the words needed to complete the paragraph. Some words will not be used.

unimpeachable	exegesis	otiose	renunciation
puerile	pander	recalcitrant	

1. The defense attorney's _____ efforts to win the trial simply delayed the inevitable; the _____ evidence had quickly convinced the jury that the defendant was guilty. When the verdict was read, the defendant, a former executive, shocked courtroom observers with _____ remarks. Bailiffs then dragged the _____ prisoner from the courtroom, while he kicked and clawed at any court official within reach.

    "The defendant's blatant _____ of the law," said the judge, "demands a strict reprisal, which will be determined at the sentencing hearing tomorrow."

From the list below, supply the words needed to complete the paragraph. Some words will not be used.

aleatory	ameliorate	profligate	exegesis
inveigh	otiose	asperity	

2. Tina liked her new first-floor apartment, but she couldn't stand the _____ upstairs tenants, who partied incessantly though the night, keeping everyone awake. After enduring several days of nonstop music and stomping, Tina visited the noisy neighbor and spoke with a[n] _____ she usually reserved for dealing with the most difficult of people.

    "You shouldn't require a[n] _____ of the lease to know that it's not proper to disturb every tenant in the building with your noise!" screamed Tina, in order to be heard over the blaring stereo. The offending neighbor simply closed the door, leaving Tina standing in the hall alone. During the week that followed, Tina encouraged her other neighbors to call the landlord and _____ against the habits of the noisy tenants so as to _____ the living conditions of the apartment building.

From the list below, supply the words needed to complete the paragraph. Some words will not be used.

pander	lionize	unimpeachable	aleatory
vitiate	allay	asperity	

3.   The world of pop culture _____ the talk-radio host for his racy programs, but thousands of angry listeners claimed that his low humor and poorly supported arguments simply _____ the younger generations of listeners. The host, they claimed, _____ to the young by supplying their vivid imaginations with scenarios that defy traditional morality. Raising children properly is _____ enough, they argued, without adding counterproductive distractions. Network executives held a meeting, and in the following week, the network attempted to _____ the angry listeners by rescheduling the show to a late-night slot.

EXERCISE II—Sentence Completion

Complete the sentence in a way that shows you understand the meaning of the italicized vocabulary word.

1.   Dan's *otiose* attempt to ski resulted in…

2.   Ryan read an *exegesis* of the cryptic poem because…

3.   Some citizens feared that the new casino would *vitiate*…

4.   The man *pandered* to concert fans by selling T-shirts for twenty dollars each, even though he…

5.   The *profligate* senator was voted out shortly after…

6.   Teresa *inveighed* against the proposed landfill because…

7.   Ted thought that firing more people would *ameliorate* the company's finances, but instead…

8.   The criminal mistakenly thought that the public would *lionize* him if he…

9.   The professor expected *puerile* comments from four-year-olds, but not…

10. It took three hours to convince the *recalcitrant* fugitive to…

11. The inmate failed to convince the parole board of his complete *renunciation* of...

12. Harvey had an *unimpeachable* belief in ghosts after...

13. To *allay* the pain of your headache, you might...

14. The drill sergeant claimed that her *asperity* was necessary because it...

15. The baseball player made an *aleatory* promise to the sick youngster that he would...

EXERCISE III—Roots, Prefixes, and Suffixes

Study the entries and answer the questions that follow.

The roots *nat* and *nasc* mean "to be born."
The root *viv* means "to live."
The root *mort* means "to die."
The prefix *con* means "together."
The prefix *pre* means "before."
The suffix *fy* means "to make."

1. *Using literal translations as guidance, define the following words without using a dictionary.*

   A. mortify   D. nascent
   B. convivial   E. vivify
   C. prenatal   F. vivid

2. A person born in a country is _____ to that country.

3. The root *sect* means "to cut apart"; *vivisection*, therefore, literally means _____ .

4. What does a *mortician* do for a living?

5. List as many words as you can think of that contain the root *viv*.

EXERCISE IV—Inference

Complete the sentences by inferring information about the italicized word from its context.

1. Your motives must be *unimpeachable* if you plan to attempt something that...

2. Someone might *inveigh* against your plan if...

3. A *recalcitrant* child might refuse to...

EXERCISE V—Critical Reading

Below is a pair of reading passages followed by several multiple-choice questions similar to the ones you will encounter on the SAT. Carefully read both passages and choose the best answer to each of the questions.

The authors of the following passages offer two different perspectives on the significance of the Internet.

Passage 1

From protecting American lives to enriching the lives of people all over the world, the Internet stands as one of the greatest collaborative inventions of all time. In 1969, the Pentagon sponsored a network of computers at four major universities, creating a system that allowed the United States military to communicate and
5 maintain control over missiles during a simulated nuclear war. Researchers named the network ARPANET after the Advanced Research Projects Agency, a military technological think-tank. By the early seventies, thirty-seven computers communicated with each other via ARPANET. Ironically, what began as an effort to control the chaos of a nuclear holocaust soon morphed into a happy, chaotic world of its
10 own.

Beginning in 1972 with the invention of electronic mail, ARPANET also functioned as a high-speed post office. At the First International Conference on Computers and Communication held in Washington, D.C., demonstrations of the network in action stimulated interest and research, and soon many more networks
15 appeared. In 1974, researchers began using a common language, Transmission Control Protocol and Internet Protocol (TCP/IP), that allowed the networks to communicate with each other. Stanford University researchers introduced a commercial version of ARPANET that same year, and they officially dubbed the ever-expanding network, the "Internet." In the years since, schools, libraries, hospitals,
20 and corporations hurried to connect to the Net; thus, the Internet revolutionized society's way of learning and sharing information.

Today, the Information Superhighway (as the Net was slugged to generate interest in Al Gore's 1991 High Performance Computing Act) entices everyone to cruise its main drags and back roads; computer companies and Internet service providers
25 boast incredible features at affordable prices, making it easier than ever to merge into the fast lane. Combined with incredible video technology, the Internet offers casual users a scenic route for their information road trip, on which they can enjoy the picturesque view of vacation spots, pictures from the grandchildren, or the photographic evidence that the perfect chocolate cake recipe really does exist.
30　Educators and their students use the Internet's many reputable news and reference sites to access valuable information. Scientists still use the Internet, only now they can communicate text, pictures, and movie footage with scientists all over the world. Medical professionals exchange life-saving information with each other, and post that information for patient access. Gone are the days when the Internet
35 belonged solely to military scientists and university researchers. The road less traveled has become the main thoroughfare, and to be without access has become quite pedestrian.

Passage 2

Created in the 1960s to protect America in the aftermath of a nuclear attack, the Internet now threatens to destroy the nation, slowly, insidiously, and completely. Rather than nuclear explosions, Americans face Internet-induced implosion that will cause morals and values to crumble and decay in the dust of apathy.
5 Independent intelligent thought will go up in a nauseating, miasmic mushroom cloud of muddled misinformation, and relationships and community will cease altogether.

Since the Internet, born of a partnership between government and academia, became available to ordinary citizens, people no longer use libraries, encyclopedias,
10 or their own brains to solve problems. When boredom strikes and an original idea does not, people surf the sea of mediocrity known as the World Wide Web. They accept as truth everything they see there. They dismiss their powers of logic and common sense in favor of following blindly the simulacrum-strewn path of Internet misinformation. Thus, overuse and abuse of the Internet promotes banal-
15 ity of thought, slovenliness of research habits, and sheer idiocy of behavior.

Young people are especially susceptible to the propagation of half-truths and myths found on the Internet. The Internet hampers their ability to focus by constantly interrupting with pop-up advertisements and instant messages begging for response. Students cannot concentrate and become frustrated; after all, fact check-
20 ing and attribution take time. Today's young people are growing up accustomed to instant gratification; that is precisely why the Internet appeals to them. Meanwhile, plagiarism is becoming commonplace as students attempt to download instant good grades, even if the source belongs to someone else.

Furthermore, the Internet promotes hate, and hate unchecked decimates faster
25 than the Black Death. Prejudice prevails thanks to a plethora of propaganda-based websites espousing ethnic and cultural superiority. Even the most ignorant cretin

can post on any number of Internet locations with malicious intent and simultaneous impunity. Hatemongers remain anonymous by using screen names, web pseudonyms that cannot be traced; thus, these insolent Internet users partici-
30 pate in on-line anarchy, avoiding censorship, regulation, and accountability. Internet induced-and-abetted hate crimes and acts of terrorism are sure to follow.

Many people amusingly harbor the illusion that the Internet is a valuable tool used by upstanding citizens strictly in the pursuit of professional and personal excellence. Apparently, "personal excellence" must have been redefined over the
35 past decade: the Internet is a virtual altar at which millions of sex addicts faithfully worship. Over 260 million pages of pornography clog the web, and computer prostitutes abound. Common sense holds, and statistics prove, that Internet pornography contributes to marital problems and the increasing divorce rate; yet even so-called respectable members of society use the Internet to indulge their perversions.
40 Certainly, the mere thought of a gentle family practitioner or a beloved elementary-school teacher engaging in such lewd pursuits should generate concern; however, moral decay flourishes in an atmosphere of apathy, a byproduct of the Internet.

Spending a lot of time online (regardless of the activity pursued) also leads to isolationism and the deterioration of social relationships. Who needs to visit
45 friends when an e-mail will suffice? Who needs to attend religious services when groups can worship online? Virtual communities fill the emptiness with pseudo-socialization that requires no commitment, laying waste to real families and real neighborhoods. Lazy consumers no longer need to leave the house to shop. Slacking singles can go on virtual dates that require no preparation. Uninformed
50 patients can visit web doctors for dubious professional opinions, sight unseen. Soon, a generation of children with bold, gregarious chat room personalities will refuse to leave their own homes because they might be required—it's frightening—to speak to an actual stranger in person.

The Internet monster shall soon have thrust its tentacles into every aspect of
55 American life, weakening the nation from the inside out. From horoscopes to horror films to horticulture, everything will exist digitally, and Internet-induced agoraphobia will reduce this nation to a collective of pale, atrophied, hermits who buy groceries, go to college, get married, and have children online.

1. According to passage 1, researchers developed the Internet to
   A. enrich lives through enhanced communication.
   B. send e-mail from universities to military bases.
   C. assist medical research.
   D. provide a cheap means of intercollegiate communication.
   E. maintain control of weapons after a nuclear attack.

2. In paragraph 3 of passage 1, the author uses a metaphor to
   A. foreshadow the expansion of the Internet.
   B. compare the Internet to a highway.
   C. add humor to the passage.
   D. explain how language changes to reflect technology.
   E. personify the Internet.

3. As used in line 21 of passage 1, the term *slugged* most nearly means
   A. struck.
   B. hit with a bat.
   C. named.
   D. fought.
   E. tagged.

4. Which of the following best describes the tone of passage 1?
   A. light and informative
   B. comical and humorous
   C. critical and judgmental
   D. technical and authoritative
   E. biased and dogmatic

5. In line 14 of passage 2, the word *sheer* most nearly means
   A. transparent.
   B. to slice.
   C. to turn off course.
   D. unmitigated.
   E. very steep.

6. In passage 2, line 25, the word *cretin* most nearly means
   A. innocent person.
   B. idiotic person.
   C. hindered person.
   D. silly person.
   E. physically disabled person.

7. In paragraphs 1 and 4 of the second passage, the author uses a series of words that begin with the same sounds. The author uses this alliteration in order to
   A. make the paragraph read like a poem.
   B. impart an encoded message to readers.
   C. personify the Internet.
   D. demonstrate the language of anonymous chat rooms.
   E. emphasize the condemning tone of the paragraph.

8. The tone of passage 2 is
   A. encouraging and supportive.
   B. mildly critical.
   C. judgmental and contentious.
   D. educational and informative.
   E. light and humorous.

9. The authors of both passages would agree that
   A. the Internet should be abolished.
   B. military researchers developed the Internet.
   C. the Internet should be celebrated.
   D. the Internet has a bright future.
   E. the Internet is a threat to the American public.

10. Which statement most accurately describes both passages?
    A. Passage 1 is argumentative, and passage 2 is objective.
    B. Passage 1 and passage 2 were written by the same author.
    C. Passage 1 is likely to appear in a newspaper.
    D. Both passages are informal.
    E. Both passages are scholarly.

Lesson Nine

1. **provocative** (prə vok´ ə tiv) *adj.* tending to excite or stimulate
   The daughter considered her mother's short skirt too *provocative*.
   syn: provoking; exciting   *ant: dull; boring*

2. **bumpkin** (bump´ kin) *n.* an unsophisticated, awkward person
   Pickpockets often prey on *bumpkins* who forget to protect their wallets
   while visiting the city.
   syn: yokel; hayseed; rube   *ant: intellectual*

3. **toady** (tō´ dē) *n.* a person who flatters for personal gain
   The *toady* followed the young queen around, agreeing with every idiotic
   statement she uttered.
   syn: sycophant; flatterer

4. **culpable** (kul´ pə bəl) *adj.* deserving blame or condemnation; guilty
   The prosecutor said that the crime boss was *culpable* for the murders
   even though he himself did not kill the victims.
   syn: blameworthy; liable   *ant: innocent; blameless*

5. **hortatory** (hor´ tə tōr ē) *adj.* encouraging; inciting
   The troops cheered during the general's *hortatory* speech.
   syn: exhorting   *ant: discouraging; dampening*

6. **penultimate** (pi nəl´ tə mət) *adj.* next to last
   The *penultimate* step before graduation will be passing my final
   examinations.

7. **orotund** (ôr´ ə tund) *adj.* full and rich in sound (in speech)
   The narrator of the movie advertisement spoke in a deep, *orotund* voice.
   syn: resonant; resounding   *ant: quiet; reserved*

8. **blithe** (blīth) *adj.* carefree and lighthearted
   The sight of his childhood home caused Jerry to reminisce about his
   blithe days of picking blueberries and fishing in the creek behind the
   house.
   syn: cheerful; radiant   *ant: burdened; worried; troubled*

9. **soporific** (sop ə rif´ ik) *adj.* tending to induce sleep
   I stopped reading the *soporific* novel and found a more exciting one.
   syn: somniferous; monotonous   *ant: dramatic; exciting;*
                                              stimulating

10. **pervasive** (pər vā´ siv) *adj.* permeating; spreading throughout
In two days, everyone in the small town had heard the *pervasive* rumor.
syn: sweeping; persistent   *ant: contained; restricted; limited*

11. **benign** (bi nīn´) *adj.* beneficial; favorable
She let down her guard when she saw his *benign* expression.
syn: benevolent; harmless   *ant: harmful; malevolent*

12. **frenetic** (frə net´ ik) *adj.* wildly excited
The neighbors heard the *frenetic* barks of the dog that fell into the well.
syn: frenzied; frantic   *ant: calm; composed*

13. **recrimination** (ri krim ə nā´ shən) *n.* a counteraccusation
The burglar had the nerve to express *recriminations* against the
homeowner for hitting him with a shovel.
syn: countercharge

14. **indecorous** (in dek´ ər əs) *adj.* lacking good taste; improper
The heckler made *indecorous* comments during the candidate's speech.
syn: inappropriate; vulgar   *ant: decent*

15. **corroborate** (kə rob´ ə rāt) *v.* to strengthen by adding evidence
The doctor's note *corroborated* Bill's excuse for missing a week of work.
syn: confirm; substantiate; validate   *ant: contradict*

EXERCISE I—Words in Context

From the list below, supply the words needed to complete the paragraph. Some words will not be used.

benign	soporific	indecorous	bumpkin
pervasive	corroborate	frenetic	

1. David loved to spend time with his grandparents, but he loathed the _____ drive through three hundred miles of midwestern cornfields. Halfway through the trip, Dave pulled over at a dusty little gas station for coffee and fuel. Two _____ clad in bib overalls sat in lawn chairs near the front door, staring at Dave—they didn't often see city folk at their tiny outpost. He gave a[n] _____ nod to them before placing the pump nozzle into his fuel tank; he didn't want to be _____ during his first visit to the country in years. As the ancient pump made audible "dings" to mark each gallon of gas, Dave stepped away from the car and breathed in the _____ smell of corn husks.

From the list below, supply the words needed to complete the paragraph. Some words will not be used.

frenetic	orotund	provocative	pervasive
toady	hortatory	culpable	

2. The successful novelist knew that her latest book, a[n] _____ tale of star-crossed lovers and murder-for-hire, was not her best, but her agent, a fawning _____ who simply wanted more money and fame, said it was her best writing to date. Anne knew better than to take her agent's _____ comments seriously; he was simply _____ about receiving his guaranteed dividend as stated in the contract. Anne was the one who was _____ in imparting sudden, undeserved wealth to her agent; she had prematurely signed a six-year contract before she realized that she didn't need an agent to sell her books in the first place.

From the list below, supply the words needed to complete the paragraph. Some words will not be used.

recrimination	blithe	toady	orotund
corroborate	bumpkin	penultimate	

3.   A[n] _____ group of children abandoned their game of marbles to flock around the burly man delivering a[n] _____ sales pitch from the top of a wagon in the town square. He was selling genuine musical instruments, he said, and he _____ his claims by unveiling samples of trumpets, clarinets, flutes, and even some snare drums. In response to those in the crowd who asserted that he was simply a scam artist who would take everyone's money and leave town without providing the instruments, the quick-witted man expressed insincere _____, suggesting that his accusers simply feared that the town's children might have an opportunity that their parents never had. In three days, the salesman had collected enough orders—and cash—to complete the _____ step in his plan: to get as far away from the little town as he possibly could before the people realized that they had been conned.

EXERCISE II—Sentence Completion

Complete the sentence in a way that shows you understand the meaning of the italicized vocabulary word.

1.   The child's mother became *frenetic* when…

2.   No single person is *culpable* for…

3.   Fans came from all around to hear the *orotund* voice of…

4.   The sound of the ocean had a *soporific* effect that caused…

5.   It was once considered *provocative* for people to show affection in public, but now…

6.   Without realizing the danger, the poorly informed *bumpkin* walked right into…

7.   Talking on a cellular phone is *indecorous* behavior when you are…

8.   For many people, the *penultimate* step before going to sleep at night is to…

9.   Charles looked forward to the *blithe* days he'd have during…

10. The wealthy broker grew tired of *toadies* who…

11. The teacher accused the boy of fighting, but the boy expressed *recrimination* by…

12. The villagers grabbed their pitchforks and torches after the mayor's *hortatory* rallying cries to…

13. Unless you can *corroborate* your need for additional funding, the government will…

14. During our trek through the desert, the *pervasive* dust and sand…

15. When the doctor explained that the growth was *benign*, the patient…

EXERCISE III—Roots, Prefixes, and Suffixes

Study the entries and answer the questions that follow.

The root *spir* means "to breathe."
The root *hal* means "to breathe."
The root *neur* means "nerve."
The prefix *con* means "together."
The prefix *ex* means "out."
The prefix *a* means "towards."
The suffix *osis* means "sickness," "condition," or "process."

1. *Using literal translations as guidance, define the following words without using a dictionary.*

   A. exhalation   D. halitosis
   B. conspire   E. aspire
   C. expire   F. neurosis

2. If you are said to have _____, then you are full of energy, or the "breath of life."

3. A device that helps asthma sufferers breathe is called a(n) _____.

4. If *per* means "through," then *perspire* literally means _____.

5. List as many words as you can think of that contain the prefix *ex*.

EXERCISE IV—Inference

Complete the sentences by inferring information about the italicized word from its context.

1. If no one can *corroborate* your story that you were home on the night of the burglary, the court might...

2. The inspectors at the factory will need to find the person *culpable* for the tragic explosion so they can...

3. On the school bus, the children's *frenetic* behavior caused...

EXERCISE V—Writing

Here is a writing prompt similar to the one you will find on the writing portion of the SAT.

Plan and write an essay based on the following statement:

> But, Rome, 'tis thine alone, with awful sway,
> To rule mankind, and make the world obey,
> Disposing peace and war by thy own majestic way;
> To tame the proud, the fetter'd slave to free:
> These are imperial arts, and worthy thee."

> –Virgil (70–19 B.C.)
> *Aeneid*: Chapter VI

Assignment: In the above quotation, Aeneas, the hero of Virgil's epic poem *Aeneid*, addresses the duties of newly founded Rome: to impose order, peace, and war as necessary; to free those people enslaved during the conquest to create Rome; and to "tame the proud." In an essay, explain the meaning of the phrase, "To tame the proud." To whom is Virgil alluding, and how would you feel if the President of the United States used the same language today? Support your opinion using evidence from reading, studies, current events, and your observation or experience.

Thesis: Write a one-sentence response to the above assignment. Make certain this sentence offers a clear statement of your position.

Example: Aeneas, like all great rulers, suggests that "the proud," or enemies of Rome, must be controlled if the new nation is to survive.

Organizational Plan: If your thesis is the point on which you want to end, where does your essay need to begin? List the points of development that are inevitable in leading your reader from your beginning point to your end point. This list is your outline.

Draft: Use your thesis as both your beginning and your end. Following your outline, write a good first draft of your essay. Remember to support all of your points with examples, facts, references to reading, etc.

Review and revise: Exchange essays with a classmate. Using the Holistic scoring guide on page 252, score your partner's essay (while he or she scores yours). If necessary, rewrite your essay to correct the problems indicated by the essay's score.

Identifying Sentence Errors

Identify the grammatical error in each of the following sentences. If the sentence contains no error, select answer E.

1. However hard it <u>rains, the frogs</u> in my pond <u>continue to enjoy</u>
         (A)   (B)   (C)

    <u>themselves;</u> when the<u>weather changes, though, they</u> begin to prepare for
                                         (D)

    hibernation.   <u>No error</u>
                   (E)

2. <u>Betty, who had the best average of anyone in math class, could</u> not
                         (A)

    believe her ears when the <u>teacher said, "Betty,</u> you must not have
                           (B)

    studied for this <u>test; you</u> missed half the <u>answers."</u>   <u>No error</u>
              (C)   (D)   (E)

3. The lost campers wandered through the <u>mountains, camped each</u> night
                                (A)

    wherever they <u>could, ate wild</u> berries, managed to avoid <u>bears and</u>
             (B)   (C)

    mountain <u>lions and never</u> gave up hope.   <u>No error</u>
           (D)   (E)

4. The little children chased the <u>rabbits into burrows</u> and didn't worry
                             (A)

    about <u>anything,</u> while the <u>kid's parents</u> worried about
        (B)   (C)

    <u>mosquitoes'</u> biting.   <u>No error</u>
      (D)   (E)

5. Tiffany has a <u>much larger</u> car <u>than Sheila,</u> the woman <u>who works</u> at our
             (A)   (B)   (C)

    office and <u>drives</u> a new sport utility vehicle. <u>No error</u>
          (D)   (E)

Improving Sentences

The underlined portion of each sentence below contains some flaw. Select the answer that best corrects the flaw.

6.   During the hot, dry summer, commercial farmers growing fruits and grains in low elevations recognized <u>they needed more water to survive, they installed new irrigation systems.</u>
   A.   that farmers needed more water to survive so they installed new irrigation systems.
   B.   that the plants would not survive without more water; for that reason, the farmers installed new irrigation systems.
   C.   the plant's key to survival was water, possible only with new irrigation systems.
   D.   they were going to lose the crops if no one installed new irrigation systems.
   E.   they needed more water for the plants, and the plants would not survive so they, the farmers, installed new irrigation systems.

7.   The family of doctors traces <u>their medical heritage back to the sixteen hundreds.</u>
   A.   its medical heritage to the seventeenth century.
   B.   their medical heritage back to the 1600s.
   C.   their heritage back to the seventeenth century.
   D.   medical heritage to the sixteenth century.
   E.   its medical history back to the sixteenth century.

8.   <u>Playing until one o'clock in the morning, the police were called</u> to shut down the concert.
   A.   Playing until one o'clock in the morning, someone called the police
   B.   Playing until 1:00 a.m., the police were called
   C.   At one o'clock in the morning, the police were called
   D.   By playing until one o'clock in the morning, the police were called
   E.   The police were called; someone was playing until one o'clock in the morning,

9. Because the math problems were difficult for me to do, I had forgotten all the equations.
    A. I had forgotten all the equations, because the math problems were difficult for me to complete.
    B. Because the math problems were difficult for me to do, I forgot all the equations.
    C. The math problems were difficult for me because I had forgotten to do all the equations.
    D. The math problems were difficult to do, but all the equations had been forgotten by me.
    E. The math problems were difficult to do because I had forgotten all the equations.

10. After Mr. Edwards died, workers at his company realize how much he did for the neighborhood, and they have been circulating a petition to have a street named after him.
    A. After Mr. Edwards died, workers at his company realized how much he had done for the neighborhood, and they have been circulating
    B. After Mr. Edwards has died, workers at his company have realized how much he did for the neighborhood, and, since then, they had been circulating
    C. After Mr. Edwards passed away, workers at his company realized what he did for the neighborhood and since then they have circulated
    D. When Mr. Edwards died, workers at his company, realizing how much he does for the neighborhood, had been circulating
    E. Mr. Edwards died, and workers at his company realize how much he has done for the neighborhood, and since then they have been circulating

Lesson Ten

1. **majordomo** (mā jər-dō´ mō)   *n.*   a chief butler or assistant
   The baron's *majordomo* tends the estate while his master is away.

2. **untenable** (un ten´ ə bəl)   *adj.*   impossible to defend or justify
   The judge's dismissal of the defendant's *untenable* claim was due to lack of evidence.
   syn: groundless; unsupported; indefensible   ant: sound; irrefutable

3. **perambulate** (pə ram´ byə lāt)   *v.*   to walk about; to stroll
   Though arthritic, the elderly woman could still *perambulate* among the brilliantly flowered paths of her garden.
   syn: saunter; wander

4. **veneer** (və nēr´)   *n.*   a thin, attractive layer that conceals something common or coarse
   He disguised his greed with a *veneer* of smiles and charitable words.
   syn: disguise; gloss; facade

5. **timorous** (tim´ ər əs)   *adj.*   timid
   The puppy was so small and *timorous* that all its siblings bullied it.
   syn: bashful; sheepish; reticent   ant: bold; confident; courageous

6. **luminous** (lōō´ mə nəs)   *adj.*   emitting light
   That wristwatch has *luminous* numbers so you can see them at night.
   syn: glowing; radiant   ant: dim; dark

7. **circuitous** (sər kyōō´ i təs)   *adj.*   indirect; roundabout
   The bridge flooded the highway, so we were forced to take a *circuitous* detour that added two hours to our trip.
   syn: roundabout; meandering   ant: direct; straight

8. **perquisite** (pər´ kwə zət)   *n.*   a tip or payment in addition to regular wages
   The *perquisite* of a company car offset the job's mediocre salary.
   syn: fringe benefit; perk; benefit

9. **probity** (prō´ bə tē)   *n.*   integrity; respectability
   Though still a teenager, Irene had the *probity* to be a trustworthy babysitter.
   syn: rectitude; decency; trustworthiness   ant: wickedness; impiety

10. **polemical** (pə lə´ mi kəl) *adj.* relating to controversy or argument
The mayor's *polemical* statement jeopardized his political career.
syn: controversial; contentious   *ant: indisputable; agreeable*

11. **tacit** (tas´ it) *adj.* indicated but not expressed; implied silently
Dad didn't want me to go to the concert, but he gave his *tacit* approval
by saying nothing when I asked permission to go.
syn: hinted; suggested; unspoken   *ant: explicit; frank*

12. **largesse** (lär zhes´) *n.* generosity
Building the art center would have been impossible if it were not for the
largesse of several wealthy benefactors.
syn: magnanimity; munificence   *ant: stinginess*

13. **indolent** (in´ də lənt) *adj.* lazy
The first round of firings removed *indolent* workers who looked as
though they were not working.
syn: torpid; idle; lethargic   *ant: industrious; busy; productive*

14. **circumlocution** (sûr kəm lō kyōō´ shən) *n.* unnecessarily wordy or
evasive language
When the teacher asked about her progress on the science project, the
student's *circumlocution* revealed that she had not even begun it.
syn: discursiveness; indirectness; evasion   *ant: conciseness; brevity*

15. **depredate** (dep ri dāt´) *v.* to plunder and pillage
During the riot, revelers *depredated* the banks and museums.
syn: pilfer; ransack; ravage   *ant: enhance*

EXERCISE I—Words in Context

From the list below, supply the words needed to complete the paragraph. Some words will not be used.

largesse	luminous	probity	majordomo
perquisite	circuitous	depredate	

1.   The _____ that we associate with protective service workers, such as firemen, did not develop until the late twentieth century. Police, fire departments, and ambulance services have taken a[n] _____ route to becoming the professional organizations that we know today. Before fire departments were organized, victims relied upon the _____ of neighbors using bucket brigades to save their homes; however, sometimes that was a better option than requesting assistance from the fire department. In cities, looters among volunteer firemen sometimes _____ burning homes before the flames destroyed all the valuables and brought the buildings to the ground. If faced with fighting two fires simultaneously, fire brigades responded only to the blaze that would result in better _____ for their department. The other house was left to burn.

From the list below, supply the words needed to complete the paragraph. Some words will not be used.

depredate	polemical	circumlocution	timorous
majordomo	tacit	veneer	

2.   No one had seen the reclusive billionaire, Mr. Tanket, for months. Most people saw only Tanket's _____, who had the legal authority to make decisions on Tanket's behalf. Even during a[n] _____ merger that resulted in thousands of layoffs, Mr. Tanket was not to be found. Some speculated that Tanket's hiding was a _____ clue that he had actually passed away and that the corporation was covering it up. When asked about it, representatives offered only _____ that changed the subject and failed to answer any questions. Soon, every investigative reporter in the nation was trying to chip through the _____ that was concealing some dark secret of the corporation.

From the list below, supply the words needed to complete the paragraph. Some words will not be used.

untenable	perquisite	indolent	luminous
perambulate	timorous	veneer	

3.   Phillip knew that no one would believe his _____ story about seeing a bright, _____ object hovering over his cornfield. On the night of the sighting, Phillip tried to _____ through the field to get a closer look, but the tall cornstalks obscured his view of the object, which vanished as he neared it. Perhaps, thought Phillip, whoever was flying the object was too _____ to confront an Earthling. The other villagers heckled Phillip during breakfast at the diner on the following morning.

"If you hadn't been too _____ about harvesting your crop on time," one farmer joked, "you would have been able to wave at your moon men."

EXERCISE II—Sentence Completion

Complete the sentence in a way that shows you understand the meaning of the italicized vocabulary word.

1.   Hank worried that thieves might *depredate* his house while...

2.   The *majordomo* didn't answer the door; that was the job of...

3.   Shane thought that he deserved occasional *perquisites* because...

4.   The town was grateful for the *largesse* of the widow when...

5.   The coffee table is made of cheap fiberboard, but it has a *veneer* that...

6.   The *circuitous* marathon required participants to...

7.   Matt began a tedious *circumlocution* when...

8.   Few people agreed with Doug's *untenable* reason for...

9.   The candidate was forced to defend his own *probity* when his opponent...

10. When the red light on the camera becomes *luminous*, you will know that...

11. Sometimes, the *indolent* night watchman...

12. The angry prospector could not convince his mule to *perambulate* around...

13. The boss had made no announcements, but recent cutbacks and layoffs were *tacit* signs that...

14. Please spare us your *polemical* remarks so that we can...

15. A *timorous* person would probably not...

EXERCISE III—Roots, Prefixes, and Suffixes

Study the entries and answer the questions that follow.

The roots *pel* and *puls* mean "push."
The root *vect* means "carry."
The root *port* means "carry."
The root *com* means "together" or "with."
The prefixes *in* and *im* mean "in" or "into."
The suffix *or* means "one who does."

1. *Using literal translations as guidance, define the following words without using a dictionary.*

   A. import   D. impel
   B. comport   E. invective
   C. convection   F compel

2. A laboratory animal that is carrying a disease is called a[n] _____, but someone who carries your luggage in a hotel is called a[n] _____.

3. If you want to check the rate at which your heart is pushing blood throughout your body, you check your _____. A[n] _____ is a sudden feeling that pushes you to do something.

4. List as many words as you can think of that contain the root *port*.

EXERCISE IV—Inference

Complete the sentences by inferring information about the italicized word from its context.

1. If you can't speak for fear of being overheard, you might give someone a *tacit* message by...

2. Someone who cannot *perambulate* because of injuries to his or her legs might...

3. During a battle, soldiers might need to abandon an *untenable* position because...

EXERCISE V—Critical Reading

Below is a reading passage followed by several multiple-choice questions similar to the ones you will encounter on your SAT. Carefully read the passage and choose the best answer to each of the questions.

The following passage describes an incident involving a snake.

The day was warm and bright when I, as a teenager many years ago, walked down the camp road from the mess hall to the athletic field. A small crowd was gathering around a groundskeeper, and all the young campers were staring at the ground near the man's foot. As I approached, I heard amid the mumblings of semi-
5 concerned adolescents, "Snake!" and "Hey, there's a snake over here." Looking down, I saw the writhing mass of tensed coils nearly crushed beneath the mainte-nance man's boot. I had previously been bitten by scores of non-poisonous snakes, which didn't hurt a bit, so naturally, I had no fear of this particular one and reached toward it while telling the man to lift his foot slowly.
10 It took less than a second for the copperhead to strike and bite me twice on my left hand, directly on that tender portion between the thumb and forefinger known as the "snuff box." In the remainder of that second, the sting of self-consciousness made me blink dumbly, open-mouthed—that sting of embarrassment that often accompanies a feat of stupidity. I watched as a knot about the size of an egg formed
15 on my hand; this snake, now being ground into the gravel beneath Ed the groundskeeper's steel-toed boot, was definitely not a harmless reptile. I walked slowly to the camp infirmary, staring agape at the lump on my hand. Somehow, maybe from a flyer on the camp bulletin board, maybe from a past adventure comic book, I remembered that panic and rapid movement caused venom to circulate
20 more quickly, so I made it a point to overcome my instinct to run, screaming, with my arms flailing overhead.
Luckily it was Wednesday, so Larry, the camp doctor, was in the infirmary lodge.

He immersed my hand in hot water (which I later learned was the wrong thing to do), told me to stay still, and then he left for about twenty minutes while I stood
25   there listening to my heart thump faster with the thought of going blind, or convulsing, or whatever it was that this snake's venom was going to do to me. Larry returned with a scalpel, of all things, and the sunlight coming through the open doorway glinted off the blade in a warming way. The pain began in earnest now, and it was the start of the worst agony imaginable; I would later describe it as hav-
30   ing my hand in a red-hot vise. The doctor made four small incisions over the fang marks. I eventually found out that during the time Larry was gone, Ed, who had killed the snake, was looking in an encyclopedia to determine what kind of snake it was. The swelling crept slowly up my arm, and just seeing it made it hurt more. There was no antivenin available, so Larry called an ambulance to take me to a
35   nearby hospital where some could be administered. Now I panicked.

I started to cry from the indescribable pain. Sweat and fright oozed out of me, out of each pore. I couldn't believe that I was going to become one of those people I read about—that kid who died for being so stupid. I heard the ambulance's siren, which gave me an iota of hope, but oh, the ordeal was far from over, and there was
40   lots of suffering to be had.

I tried to walk to the door to see the ambula–and oh! I fainted, and what momentary bliss it was. Larry had lifted me from beneath my arms and began dragging me outside when I woke up again, and the pain had increased exponentially, as punishment for the temporarily relief of unconsciousness. In the ambulance, the seri-
45   ous look of the paramedic reminded me to panic, but not as much as his ordering the driver to "Step on it! This kid's in trouble!" During the fast ride, my swollen arm seemed to absorb the shock of every tiny bump that that steel-wheeled wagon of an ambulance ran over. After what felt like hours of torture, the rear doors flew open and the two paramedics shuffled me to gurney as I grunted and howled simul-
50   taneously.

In the emergency room, through eyes welling with tears of pain, I caught a blurred glimpse of a grave-looking doctor holding what appeared to be some kind of gigantic, novelty syringe filled with yellow liquid. Before I had the chance to protest, he sank the needle into an arm so swollen that I didn't even recognize when
55   I looked down. I yelped, choking on my own screams as the throbbing pain skyrocketed. "Stop it! Make it stop!" I moaned in agony, through clenched, grinding teeth. Then, through squinted eyes, I saw my mother, or so I thought, standing next to the gurney. "Don't worry," she said. Unfortunately, it didn't calm me or lessen the pain, so I continued to scream, my throat now getting hoarse. After yet another
60   interminable period of recoiling and howling, I was pinned down by the doctor long enough for him to inject some kind of painkiller, and finally, the pain subsided and I drifted off into a fitful sleep.

I woke up the next day—literally, the next day. I slept for twenty-four hours, and miraculously, the pain was gone. There were, however, a few after-effects. When I
65   looked down, I found an arm three-times the diameter of the one that had been there the day before; it looked like a bodybuilder's arm, but it was impossible to bend it. My left hand looked ridiculous: it was twice its normal size, and it had three large blisters on it, each the size of a ping-pong ball. The swelling stretched the whole way to my neck. It took a week of physical therapy to get my arm
70   moving again.

My family had arrived during the night while I slept uneasily, and they told me that I had been critical for a long while. Later in the week, while I exercised my arm by tugging on a nylon bungee cord tied to the bed rail, Larry visited and brought me snakeskin mounted on a board. It was an amazing forty-three inches long.

75   Now, many years after my learning experience, I still can't flatten my left hand. Perhaps when I figure out why I tried to grab that snake in the first place, I'll figure out how to move my hand again. Until that time, I'll just call Ed if I see a snake.

1. The main purpose of this passage is
   A. to warn people to avoid snakes.
   B. to explain medical procedures for a snakebite.
   C. to describe a personal memory.
   D. to demonstrate how youth believes itself to be invincible.
   E. to warn against incompetent doctors.

2. The overall tone or mood of this passage is best described as
   A. reflective.
   B. humorous.
   C. speculative.
   D. irresponsible.
   E. blameful.

3. Which choice best explains why the author included the following sentence?

   > Larry returned with a scalpel, of all things, and the sunlight coming through the open doorway glinted off the blade in a warming way.

   A. The author is suggesting that the scalpel is very sharp.
   B. The description foreshadows the trip to the hospital.
   C. The author is using irony to suggest the sight of the scalpel is frightening.
   D. The scalpel is a symbol of the author's rite of passage.
   E. The author is explaining why the doctor is described as insane.

4. The word *antivenin* in line 34 most nearly means
   A. some type of poison.
   B. anti-pain.
   C. medication for infection.
   D. strong tranquilizer.
   E. something to counteract poison.

5. In paragraph 3, what purpose does the disjointed time frame serve?
   A. It is unintentionally confusing.
   B. The paragraph is intended to show that the author is still alive.
   C. It is purposely jumbled to confuse the reader.
   D. It heightens the confusion of the actual incident.
   E. There is no reason for it.

6. According to the passage, the author has a hallucination in which
   A. he rides in a wagon.
   B. he sees a giant syringe.
   C. he picks up a poison snake.
   D. he sees his mother.
   E. he sees a doctor named Larry.

7. In paragraph 6, the word *interminable* most nearly means
   A. apparent.
   B. quick.
   C. awkward.
   D. unending.
   E. regretful.

8. According to the passage, which is *not* one of the things that the author experienced?
   A. vomiting
   B. passing out
   C. swelling
   D. fear
   E. blisters

9. This passage would probably be found in
   A. a book on snakes.
   B. a diary.
   C. a book report.
   D. an outdoor magazine.
   E. a conservation science journal.

10. Ed is
    A. the author.
    B. the doctor.
    C. the groundskeeper.
    D. the paramedic.
    E. the kid who found the snake.

Lesson Eleven

1. **canard**   (kə närd´)   n.   a deliberately misleading story
   The thief used the *canard* of his car's being broken down to lure victims into the alley.
   syn: lie; pretense; sham   *ant: fact; truth; reality*

2. **wont**   (wont)   *adj.*   likely
   Be careful: that dog is *wont* to bite strangers.
   syn: accustomed

3. **etymology**   (et ə mol´ ə jē)   n.   the history of a word; the study of word origins
   If you trace the *etymology* of the word "khaki," you will find that it comes from the Persian word for "dust."

4. **cortege**   (kôr tezh´)   n.   a group of attendants; a retinue
   The royal *cortege* filled every room of a hotel floor during the queen's visit.
   syn: entourage; followers; posse

5. **solecism**   (sä´ lə si zəm)   n.   a deviation or error in speech, manners, or deeds
   Using the word "less" instead of "fewer" when referring to individual items is a common *solecism*.
   syn: mistake; faux pas; blunder

6. **demotic**   (di mot´ ik)   *adj.*   relating to ordinary people
   The nuclear physicist had trouble explaining his theories in *demotic* language.
   syn: colloquial; common   *ant: formal; elevated*

7. **simian**   (si´ mē ən)   *adj.*   related to or resembling an ape or monkey
   The photograph of the alleged Bigfoot showed a *simian* creature walking upright through the forest.

8. **impresario**   (im pri sär´ ē ō)   n.   an entertainment producer or manager
   The *impresario* of the concert hall had to book the famous soloist two years in advance.
   syn: organizer; proprietor

9. **requisite** (rek´ wi zit) *adj.* required; necessary
Glenn's loan application was rejected because he omitted some *requisite* information.
syn: imperative; needed; important   *ant: incidental; nonessential*

10. **bulwark** (bul´ wərk) *n.* a defensive wall or embankment
Residents constructed a *bulwark* of sandbags to protect the town from the rising tide.
syn: fortification; barrier

11. **malaise** (ma lāz´) *n.* vague bodily or emotional discomfort or uneasiness
Tina could tell by her own *malaise* that she had contracted her daughter's cold.
syn: illness; distress; discontent   *ant: comfort; relief; peace*

12. **disingenuous** (dis in jen´ ōō əs) *adj.* insincere; calculating
The *disingenuous* used car salesman pointed out the car's new paint job, but not that the car had been a taxicab.
syn: duplicitous; cunning; shifty   *ant: honest; sincere; candid*

13. **crescendo** (krə shen´ dō) *n.* a gradual increase in intensity, force, or volume
The two-week city police strike resulted in a *crescendo* of crime.
syn: increase; buildup   *ant: decrease; waning*

14. **intransigent** (in tran´ sə jənt) *adj.* uncompromising; refusing to moderate
The *intransigent* man would rather go to prison than pay income taxes.
syn: determined; immovable; obdurate   *ant: flexible; yielding*

15. **dogged** (dô´ gid) *adj.* unrelenting; persistent
Obsessed with his experiment, the *dogged* scientist locked himself in his laboratory and worked for three days with little rest.
syn: driven; steadfast; unwavering   *ant: hesitating; vacillating*

EXERCISE I—Words in Context

From the list below, supply the words needed to complete the paragraph. Some words will not be used.

canard	requisite	bulwark	dogged
simian	crescendo	intransigent	

1. The Colonel had explained that it was _____ for the platoon to hold the line that night, and, despite taking heavy casualties, the _____ soldiers repelled the overwhelming enemy forces as ordered. Eventually, a[n] _____ in the enemy's offensive forced McIntyre and Carson to abandon their foxhole and retreat to the _____, where the rest of the platoon had taken cover. The retreat was not an easy task: bullets and shrapnel whizzed by the _____ soldiers as they leapt over bushes, dodged trees, and crawled through open areas in an attempt to evade enemy fire.

From the list below, supply the words needed to complete the paragraph. Some words will not be used.

wont	cortege	crescendo	impresario
disingenuous	canard	demotic	

2. Bernadette, the most sought-after singer in the music industry, hired a[n] _____ assistant who was talented at fabricating believable _____ in order to mislead the nosy reporters and paparazzi. Bernadette, unlike many stars, did not travel with a _____ comprising makeup artists, groupies, and bodyguards, so it was easier for her to avoid tabloid reporters and mobs of fans. Despite having amassed a fortune after her latest album went platinum, Bernadette did not buy a mansion or a fleet of cars; she simply tried to live the _____ life to which she was accustomed. She routinely rejected the offers of the most prominent _____ in the entertainment industry, who in turn threatened to take her fame away as fast as she gained it. Bernadette usually responded with a simple, "Go ahead."

From the list below, supply the words needed to complete the paragraph. Some words will not be used.

wont   bulwark   etymology   solecism
demotic   simian   malaise

3.   Bobby was pale this morning and obviously suffering from some sort of
_____, but by the afternoon, he was back to performing his
_____ antics and driving his mother to the brink of insanity. The
weather was _____ to improve soon, so Bobby could then take his
energy to the back yard, where there were fewer things to break.

"Mommy, I was sick this morning, but I'm feeling gooder now." Jane corrected her son's _____:

"You're feeling *better* now."

"That's what I just said," said Bobby as the long leaves of a houseplant caught his attention. Jane shook her head. She didn't care if Bobby knew the _____ of every word he spoke, but she definitely wanted him to speak well.

EXERCISE II—Sentence Completion

Complete the sentence in a way that shows you understand the meaning of the italicized vocabulary word.

1. The *dogged* rescue workers spent hours trying to...

2. The father remained *intransigent* when his daughter asked...

3. Hoping to create a *crescendo* of tourism, the governor...

4. The clever villain had a *disingenuous* plan to...

5. To determine the cause of her *malaise*, Jennifer decided to...

6. The children sculpted a huge *bulwark* out of snow that would...

7. *Requisite* items for the camping trip include...

8. When the popular band canceled its show, the *impresario* had to...

9. The strange rodent had *simian* characteristics that helped it to...

10. The politician claimed that her *demotic* background would help her election because...

11. During their first encounter with the mysterious tribal leader, the vastly outnumbered explorers hoped that a *solecism* in behavior would not cause...

12. The prince's *cortege* consisted of...

13. To learn about the *etymology* of a word, you might...

14. Your houseplant is *wont* to die if you...

15. Debbie, who is a career con artist, used a *canard* to...

EXERCISE III—Roots, Prefixes, and Suffixes

Study the entries and answer the questions that follow.

The root *plic* means "fold."
The root *lig* means "connect" or "bind."
The root *solv* means "loosen."
The prefix *ex* means "out."
The prefix *re* means "back" or "again."
The prefix *ab* means "away from."
The prefix *ob* means "toward" or "against."

1. *Using literal translations as guidance, define the following words without using a dictionary.*

   A. absolve   D. resolve
   B. explicate   E. applicate
   C. oblige   F. ligament

2. The root *plex* and the suffix *ply* share the same origin as the root *plic*. List as many words as you can think of that contain the root *plex* or the suffix *ply*.

3. *Solu* is another form of *solv*. List as many words as you can think of that contain the root *solu*.

4. *Com* means "together," and it changes to *col* when placed before a word that begins with an *l*. The English word that literally means "bind together" is _____ (the suffix *ate* is a Latin ending for verbs).

5. List as many words as you can think of that contain the root *solv*.

EXERCISE IV—Inference

Complete the sentences by inferring information about the italicized word from its context.

1. If the faltering business doesn't experience a *crescendo* in sales, the company will probably…

2. Someone who omits even one *requisite* step in assembling a bicycle should not be surprised if…

3. If the amount of your paycheck is less than usual, then you will probably be *wont* to…

EXERCISE V—Writing

Here is a writing prompt similar to the one you will find on the writing portion of the SAT.

Plan and write an essay on the following statement:

"Love seeketh not itself to please,
Nor for itself hath any care,
But for another gives its ease,
And builds a heaven in hell's despair."

So sung a little Clod of Clay,
Trodden with the cattle's feet,
But a Pebble of the brook
Warbled out these metres meet:

"Love seeketh only Self to please,
To bind another to its delight,
Joys in another's loss of ease,
And builds a hell in heaven's despite."

William Blake (1757–1827)
"The Clod and the Pebble"

Assignment: In an essay, explain the message that Blake intends to impart with the poem. Assume that both the Clod and the Pebble are metaphors for two very different types of people, and describe why the physical characteristics of a clod of clay, or a pebble, reflect the type of person that each of the objects represents. Support your essay by discussing an example from literature, the arts, the sciences, current events, or your experience or observation.

In an essay, assume that both the Clod and the Pebble are metaphors for people, and describe what type of person each one must be.

Thesis: Write a one-sentence response to the above statement. Make certain this sentence offers a clear statement of your position.

Example: William Blake's poem is a reminder that there are two sides to every-thing, and people will always have varying perspectives that depend solely on personal status and life experience.

Organizational Plan: If your thesis is the point on which you want to end, where does your essay need to begin? List the points of development that are inevitable in leading your reader from your beginning point to your end point. This is your outline.

Draft: Use your thesis as both your beginning and your end. Following your outline, write a good first draft of your essay. Remember to support all of your points with examples, facts, references to reading, etc.

Review and revise: Exchange essays with a classmate. Using the scoring guide for Organization on page 248, score your partner's essay (while he or she scores yours). Focus on the organizational plan and the use of language conventions. If necessary, rewrite your essay to improve the organizational plan and your use of language.

Improving Paragraphs

Read the following passage and then answer the multiple-choice questions that follow. The questions will require you to make decisions regarding the revision of the reading selection.

(1) If someone asked you which professional sport has the most interesting athletes, what would you say? (2) Terrell Owens, Deion Sanders and even Terry Bradshaw hail from the National Football League. (3) Larry Bird, Michael Jordan, and Shaquille O'Neill all play hoops. (4) The fiery tempers of Eddie Belfour, Jeremy Roenick, and Marty McSorley exist only on ice rinks. (5) But what about baseball? (6) Baseball is a sport usually played in the summer. (7)Most professional baseball players seem to portray relaxed demeanors, and the nature of the sport disallows the extremes that one might observe at a football game or a rugby match; however, one of the most unusual personalities ever to play sports did play baseball, and his name was Jimmy Piersall.

(8) Unfortunately, Jimmy's rookie season was cut short by a nervous breakdown, which gave him a reputation for mental instability that followed him throughout his career. (9) Piersall began his major league baseball career in 1952 with the Boston Red Sox. (10) In 1950 and 1951, Piersall compiled batting averages of .346 and .339 respectively for Boston's minor league team in Birmingham, Alabama; however, Piersall was a centerfielder for Birmingham, and the Red Sox already had a major league star in center field—Dom DiMaggio, brother of the legendary Joe DiMaggio. (11) Piersall switched to shortstop so that he could join the major league club, but Piersall's accomplishments on the field were overshadowed by his erratic, albeit laughable, behavior.

(12) Despite Piersall's relative success at bat, his crazy behavior made headlines more often than his statistics did. (13) During his rookie year, Piersall made waves by brawling with New York Yankee Billy Martin in the clubhouse tunnel. (14) From 1953 onward, Jimmy stood out as a ballplayer by racking up hits and home runs, but his reputation of eccentricity continued to follow him. (15) On July 23, 1960, the day after a game in which Jimmy hit two home runs, he was ejected from a game for an unusual reason. (16) During two of Ted Williams' at-bats for Boston, Piersall, then playing for Cleveland performed a "war dance" in center field meant to distract Williams. (17) The umpires tolerated Jimmy's clowning until the eighth inning before they ejected him. (18) This, however, was not the most infamous incident in Piersall's career.

(19) Jimmy Piersall hit only one home run while playing in the National League. (20) But most of his career was spent with the Red Sox, the Indians, and the California Angels, his most famous home run was the one he hit with the New York Mets—also the 100th of his career. (21) After Jimmy watched the ball leave the stadium, he ran around the bases backwards, which successfully irritated both Jimmy's manager and the baseball commissioner, not to mention the opposing pitcher. (22) A few days later, the Mets released Piersall, and he signed with his last team, the Angels.

(23) Athletes like Babe Ruth, Magic Johnson, Wayne Gretzky, and Emmitt Smith, will be remembered for their accomplishments on the courts, fields, and

rinks where their sports are played. (24) Records for home runs, batting averages, points per game, rushing yards, in the memories of true sports fans. (25) Other athletes will be remembered in other ways—the ways in which their unorthodox mannerisms amuse and bewilder fans. (26) Jimmy Piersall was an eccentric and memorable personality both on and off the field, and his name will long be a diverting chapter in the annals of baseball.

1. Which sentence should be removed from paragraph 1?
    A. sentence 1
    B. sentence 2
    C. sentence 4
    D. sentence 6
    E. sentence 7

2. Which change best improves the chronology of paragraph 2?
    A. Exchange sentences 10 and 11.
    B. Move sentence 8 to the end of the paragraph.
    C. Rewrite sentence 10 in the active voice.
    D. Rewrite sentence 11 in the past perfect tense.
    E. Exchange sentences 8 and 10.

3. Where should a comma be placed in paragraph 3?
    A. after *waves* in sentence 13
    B. after *1953* in sentence 14
    C. after *game* in sentence 15
    D. after *Cleveland* in sentence 16
    E. after *clowning* in sentence 17

4. Which correction best corrects a word usage error in paragraph 4?
    A. Move *only* to follow *Piersall* in sentence 19.
    B. Replace *But* with *Although* in sentence 20.
    C. Exchange sentences 21 and 22.
    D. Capitalize *commissioner*.
    E. Change *released* to the present tense form of the verb.

5. Paragraph 5 requires revision to correct a[n]
    A. comma splice.
    B. run-on sentence.
    C. fragment.
    D. faulty parallelism.
    E. pronoun-noun agreement error.

Lesson Twelve

1. **propensity** (prə pen´ si tē) *n.* a tendency
    Sheila nurtured her *propensity* for hiking by relocating to the mountains.
    syn: inclination; predisposition; penchant   *ant: aversion*

2. **condescending** (kon di send´ ing) *adj.* displaying superiority; patronizing
    The young employee never grew accustomed to his bosses' *condescending* remarks.
    syn: denigrating; degrading   *ant: respectful; honorable*

3. **compunction** (kəm pungk´ shən) *n.* an uneasiness caused by guilt; a qualm
    Matt felt no *compunction* about stealing office supplies from work.
    syn: regret

4. **sepulcher** (se´ pəl kər) *n.* a tomb or burial chamber
    The deceased baron was placed in a foreboding *sepulcher* at the edge of the cemetery.
    syn: crypt; catacomb; mausoleum

5. **bellicose** (be´ li kōs) *adj.* warlike; inclined to fight
    Many of the crewmen were *bellicose* fellows looking for trouble.
    syn: pugnacious; belligerent; hostile   *ant: mild; passive; peaceful*

6. **pulchritude** (pəl´ krə tōōd) *n.* physical beauty
    Milton was so taken by Lauren's *pulchritude* that he couldn't respond when she greeted him.
    syn: loveliness; allure   *ant: ugliness; repulsiveness*

7. **wizened** (wiz´ ənd) *adj.* shriveled or withered from age or illness
    The *wizened* old captain had the craggy face of one who had spent a lifetime at sea.
    syn: shrunken; gnarled   *ant: sturdy; robust; stalwart*

8. **rhapsodize** (rap´ sə dīz) *v.* to express oneself enthusiastically
    She couldn't wait to go to work and *rhapsodize* about her recent engagement.
    syn: rave

9. **physiognomy** (fiz ē og´ nə mē) *n.* facial features
    His *physiognomy* revealed that he was a person who had done a lot of laughing throughout his life.
    syn: countenance; visage

10. **voluble** (vol´ yə bəl) *adj.* talkative
    The *voluble* woman was obviously comfortable speaking in front of people.
    syn: garrulous; fluent   *ant: quiet; introverted*

11. **revel** (rev´ əl) *v.* to enjoy; to take pleasure in
    The home team *reveled* in the glory of winning the championship.
    syn: bask; delight; indulge   *ant: grieve; lament*

12. **umbrage** (um´ brij) *n.* feeling of offense; resentment
    Widespread *umbrage* at the new law prompted legislators to re-evaluate it.
    syn: displeasure; ire; anger   *ant: delight; pleasure*

13. **epiphany** (i pif´ ə nē) *n.* a revelation; sudden knowledge or insight
    During an *epiphany*, John realized what he had been doing wrong throughout most of his adult life.

14. **assiduous** (ə sij´ ōō əs) *adj.* diligent; persistent
    The *assiduous* builder finally completed his home after six years of construction.
    syn: persevering; industrious   *ant: lazy; negligent*

15. **panacea** (pan ə sē´ ə) *n.* a cure-all; a remedy for all diseases
    Some grandmothers believe that chicken soup is a *panacea* for almost any ailment.
    syn: elixir; nostrum

EXERCISE I—Words in Context

From the list below, supply the words needed to complete the paragraph. Some words will not be used.

bellicose	physiognomy	wizened	condescending
sepulcher	umbrage	rhapsodize	

1. My _____ grandfather Sam had lost his eyesight years ago, but that did not affect his ability to _____ about politics as long as someone was around to listen; however, as age took his health, he became _____ toward anyone who he thought treated him in a[n] _____ way. He knew, deep down, that his failing health was a part of the natural order of things, but he took _____ at the attempts of nurses or children to help him when he really didn't need help.

From the list below, supply the words needed to complete the paragraph. Some words will not be used.

physiognomy	bellicose	pulchritude	panacea
revel	propensity	assiduous	

2. Aunt Carol, who had the grace and _____ of a ballerina when she was younger, believes that cucumber paste is a[n] _____ that clears up any wrinkles or blemishes. Each morning and night, the _____ woman applies the slimy paste, lets it set for an hour, and then removes it, half expecting to see the _____ of a twenty-year-old returning her stare from the mirror. Though disappointed daily, Carol _____ in the belief that perhaps the miracle paste just needs a few more weeks before it begins to have an effect.

From the list below, supply the words needed to complete the paragraph. Some words will not be used.

epiphany	rhapsodize	compunction	sepulcher
revel	propensity	voluble	

3.   Dr. Ramus had a[n] _____ for being in the right place at the right time, but he was in total disbelief when his team unearthed the ancient _____ rumored to contain the remains of one of the greatest rulers in history. Upon sight of the limestone slab, the normally _____ professor fell silent, unable to respond to the questions of his many assistants. He experienced a brief _____ as he gazed at the markings on the stone; somehow everything leading up to the discovery—the many letdowns and roadblocks—seemed to make sense. Now, after discovering the equivalent of the Holy Grail for his field of study, the doctor had no _____ about desecrating the ancient tomb by opening it in the name of science.

EXERCISE II—Sentence Completion

Complete the sentence in a way that shows you understand the meaning of the italicized vocabulary word.

1.   Though he had worked in an office for the last ten years, Bert had the *physiognomy* of...

2.   Marcy, obsessed with her own *pulchritude*, spent hours...

3.   Applicants for the telemarketing job cannot have any *compunction* about...

4.   Some people believe that aloe is a natural *panacea* for...

5.   Jodi hoped to have an *epiphany* in which she...

6.   The *voluble* child was always ready to...

7.   After seeing the students' test results, the teacher *rhapsodized* about...

8.   Luke's *propensity* for drawing helped him to become...

9.   The mountain climber stopped to *revel* in the...

10. Your *condescending* attitude makes it appear as though you...

11. When thousands of viewers took *umbrage* at the new sitcom, the network executives...

12. In the ancient *sepulcher*, the archaeologist found...

13. With long, continuous, *assiduous* effort, anyone can...

14. The family waited for their *wizened* grandfather to...

15. Tom has been extremely *bellicose* ever since the day...

EXERCISE III—Roots, Prefixes, and Suffixes

Study the entries and answer the questions that follow.

The root *lex* means "word."
The root *leg* means "to read."
The root *script* means "write."
The suffix *graph* means "writing."
The prefix *dys* means "bad" or "difficult."
The prefix *in* means "in" or "not."
The suffix *ion* means "the act of."

1. *Using literal translations as guidance, define the following words without using a dictionary.*

   A. lexicography   D. dyslexic
   B. illegible   E. lexicon
   C. inscription   F. script

2. Sulla, a brutal dictator of ancient Rome, invented a method of writing the names of his enemies and publishing them before (*pro* means "before") all citizens; enemies on his list were marked for punishment or death. What is the word for this act of writing and publishing? Hint: the suffix *graph* is Greek; Romans spoke in Latin.

3. The root *pep* means "to digest." What is another word that means *indigestion* or "bad digestion"?

4. What form of carbon gets its name from its use as a material used for writing?

5. List as many words as you can think of that contain the root *script*.

6. List as many words as you can think of that contain the prefix *dys*.

EXERCISE IV—Inference

Complete the sentences by inferring information about the italicized word from its context.

1. A mediocre player might take *umbrage* at the coach's decision to...

2. Someone with a *propensity* for making people laugh might consider...

3. If you are an *assiduous* student, you usually...

EXERCISE V—Critical Reading

Below is a pair of reading passages followed by several multiple-choice questions similar to the ones you will encounter on the SAT. Carefully read both passages and choose the best answer to each of the questions.

The first passage is an excerpt from "Walking," an essay written in 1862 by Henry David Thoreau (1817-1862). In the passage, Thoreau reflects upon one of the greatest freedoms available to humankind: walking in nature.

Passage 2 is Francis Bacon's essay, "Of Travel." In the essay, Bacon (1561-1626), an intellectual, philosopher, and master of English prose, offers advice about travel abroad.

Passage 1

My vicinity affords many good walks; and though for so many years I have walked almost every day, and sometimes for several days together, I have not yet exhausted them. An absolutely new prospect is a great happiness, and I can still get this any afternoon. Two or three hours' walking will carry me to as strange a coun-
5   try as I expect ever to see. A single farmhouse which I had not seen before is some-times as good as the dominions of the King of Dahomey. There is in fact a sort of harmony discoverable between the capabilities of the landscape within a circle of ten miles' radius, or the limits of an afternoon walk, and the threescore years and ten of human life. It will never become quite familiar to you.
10 Nowadays almost all man's improvements, so called, as the building of houses, and the cutting down of the forest and of all large trees, simply deform the land-scape, and make it more and more tame and cheap. A people who would begin by burning the fences and let the forest stand! I saw the fences half consumed, their ends lost in the middle of the prairie, and some worldly miser with a surveyor look-
15 ing after his bounds, while heaven had taken place around him, and he did not see the angels going to and fro, but was looking for an old post-hole in the midst of paradise. I looked again, and saw him standing in the middle of a boggy stygian fen, surrounded by devils, and he had found his bounds without a doubt, three little stones, where a stake had been driven, and looking nearer, I saw that the Prince of
20 Darkness was his surveyor.
I can easily walk ten, fifteen, twenty, any number of miles, commencing at my own door, without going by any house, without crossing a road except where the fox and the mink do: first along by the river, and then the brook, and then the meadow and the wood-side. There are square miles in my vicinity which have no
25 inhabitant. From many a hill I can see civilization and the abodes of man afar. The farmers and their works are scarcely more obvious than woodchucks and their bur-rows. Man and his affairs, church and state and school, trade and commerce, and manufactures and agriculture, even politics, the most alarming of them all—I am pleased to see how little space they occupy in the landscape. Politics is but a nar-
30 row field, and that still narrower highway yonder leads to it. I sometimes direct the

traveler thither. If you would go to the political world, follow the great road—follow that market—man, keep his dust in your eyes, and it will lead you straight to it; for it, too, has its place merely, and does not occupy all space. I pass from it as from a bean-field into the forest, and it is forgotten. In one half-hour I can walk off
35 to some portion of the earth's surface where a man does not stand from one year's end to another, and there, consequently, politics are not, for they are but as the cigar-smoke of a man.

The village is the place to which the roads tend, a sort of expansion of the highway, as a lake of a river. It is the body of which roads are the arms and legs—a triv-
40 ial or quadrivial place, the thoroughfare and ordinary of travelers. The word is from the Latin *villa*, which together with *via*, "a way," or more anciently *ved* and *vella*, *Varro* derives from *veho*, "to carry," because the villa is the place to and from which things are carried. They who got their living by teaming were said *vellaturam facere*. Hence, too, apparently, the Latin word *vilis* and our *vile*; also *villain*. This suggests
45 what kind of degeneracy villagers are liable to. They are wayworn by the travel that goes by and over them, without traveling themselves.

Some do not walk at all; others walk in the highways; a few walk across lots. Roads are made for horses and men of business. I do not travel in them much, comparatively, because I am not in a hurry to get to any tavern or grocery or livery-sta-
50 ble or depot to which they lead. I am a good horse to travel, but not from choice a roadster. The landscape-painter uses the figures of men to mark a road. He would not make that use of my figure. I walk out into a Nature such as the old prophets and poets, Menu, Moses, Homer, Chaucer, walked in. You may name it America, but it is not America: neither Americus Vespucius, nor Columbus, nor the rest were
55 the discoverers of it. There is a truer account of it in mythology than in any history of America, so called, that I have seen.

[. . .]

At present, in this vicinity, the best part of the land is not private property; the landscape is not owned, and the walker enjoys comparative freedom. But possibly the day will come when it will be partitioned off into so-called pleasure-grounds,
60 in which a few will take a narrow and exclusive pleasure only—when fences shall be multiplied, and man-traps and other engines invented to confine men to the *public* road, and walking over the surface of God's earth shall be construed to mean trespassing on some gentleman's grounds. To enjoy a thing exclusively is commonly to exclude yourself from the true enjoyment of it. Let us improve our oppor-
65 tunities, then, before the evil days come.

What is it that makes it so hard sometimes to determine whither we will walk? I believe that there is a subtle magnetism in Nature, which if we unconsciously yield to it, will direct us aright. It is not indifferent to us which way we walk. There is a right way; but we are very liable from heedlessness and stupidity to take the
70 wrong one. We would fain take that walk, never yet taken by us through this actual world, which is perfectly symbolical of the path which we love to travel in the interior and ideal world; and sometimes, no doubt, we find it difficult to choose our direction, because it does not yet exist distinctly in our idea.

Passage 2

TRAVEL, in the younger sort, is a part of education; in the elder, a part of experience. He that travelleth into a country before he hath some entrance into the language, goeth to school, and not to travel. That young men travel under some tutor, or grave servant, I allow well; so that he be such a one that hath the language, and
5   hath been in the country before; whereby he may be able to tell them what things are worthy to be seen in the country where they go; what acquaintances they are to seek; what exercises or discipline the place yieldeth. For else young men shall go hooded, and look abroad little. It is a strange thing, that in sea voyages, where there is nothing to be seen but sky and sea, men should make diaries; but in land-travel,
10 wherein so much is to be observed, for the most part they omit it; as if chance were fitter to be registered than observation. Let diaries therefore be brought in use. The things to be seen and observed are: the courts of princes, especially when they give audience to ambassadors; the courts of justice, while they sit and hear causes; and so of consistories ecclesiastic; the churches and monasteries, with the monuments
15 which are therein extant; the walls and fortifications of cities and towns, and so the havens and harbors; antiquities and ruins; libraries; colleges, disputations, and lectures, where any are; shipping and navies; houses and gardens of state and pleasure, near great cities; armories; arsenals; magazines; exchanges; burses; warehouses; exercises of horsemanship, fencing, training of soldiers, and the like; comedies,
20 such whereunto the better sort of persons do resort; treasuries of jewels and robes; cabinets and rarities; and, to conclude, whatsoever is memorable in the places where they go. After all which the tutors or servants ought to make diligent inquiry. As for triumphs, masks, feasts, weddings, funerals, capital executions, and such shows, men need not be put in mind of them; yet are they not to be neglected. If
25 you will have a young man to put his travel into a little room, and in short time to gather much, this you must do. First, as was said, he must have some entrance into the language before he goeth. Then he must have such a servant or tutor as knoweth the country, as was likewise said. Let him carry with him also some card or book describing the country where he travelleth; which will be a good key to his
30 inquiry. Let him keep also a diary. Let him not stay long in one city or town; more or less as the place deserveth, but not long; nay, when he stayeth in one city or town, let him change his lodging from one end and part of the town to another; which is a great adamant of acquaintance. Let him sequester himself from the company of his countrymen, and diet in such places where there is good company of
35 the nation where he travelleth. Let him, upon his removes from one place to another, procure recommendation to some person of quality residing in the place whither he removeth; that he may use his favor in those things he desireth to see or know. Thus he may abridge his travel with much profit. As for the acquaintance which is to be sought in travel; that which is most of all profitable is acquaintance
40 with the secretaries and employed men of ambassadors: for so in traveling in one country he shall suck the experience of many. Let him also see and visit eminent persons in all kinds, which are of great name abroad; that he may be able to tell how the life agreeth with the fame. For quarrels, they are with care and discretion to be avoided. They are commonly for mistresses, healths, place, and words. And
45 let a man beware how he keepeth company with choleric and quarrelsome persons; for they will engage him into their own quarrels. When a traveler returneth home,

let him not leave the countries where he hath traveled altogether behind him; but maintain a correspondence by letters with those of his acquaintance which are of most worth. And let his travel appear rather in his discourse than his apparel or
50 gesture; and in his discourse let him be rather advised in his answers, than forward to tell stories; and let it appear that he doth not change his country manners for those of foreign parts; but only prick in some flowers of that he hath learned abroad into the customs of his own country.

1. The metaphor in paragraph 2 of passage 1 suggests that
   A. the devil probably set fire to the fence to harass the landowner.
   B. the man who owns the fence is selling his soul to the devil.
   C. the surveyor is angry about losing his fence to a fire.
   D. developing land is evil.
   E. the smoke from the burning fence is making the sky dark.

2. According to paragraph 4 of the first passage, the author thinks very little of
   A. the beauty of nature.
   B. undeveloped countryside.
   C. the benefits of village life.
   D. walking through woods instead of roads.
   E. simple curiosities.

3. The following quote from passage 1 best applies to which example situation?

   "To enjoy a thing exclusively is commonly to exclude yourself from the true enjoyment of it."

   A. Many people feel guilty when given the opportunity to enjoy themselves.
   B. Someone who builds a nice fence will soon fail to notice it.
   C. The wealthy squander their fortunes on wildlife conservation causes.
   D. Parks require so much work to maintain that no one gets to enjoy them.
   E. Cities build wonderful parks, but disallow people to walk on the grass.

4. In passage 1, the author's attitude toward the achievements of mankind can be described as one of
   A. dismissiveness.
   B. rudeness.
   C. contempt.
   D. joy.
   E. praise.

5. The purpose of passage 2 is
   A. to retort.
   B. to defend the reputation of Europe.
   C. to brag about wealth.
   D. to dissuade from travel.
   E. to counsel.

6. According to passage 2, which is *not* a requirement for a young person traveling abroad?
   A. fluency in the language of one's destination
   B. a book about the destination
   C. a servant or guide
   D. a means of defending oneself
   E. having a diary

7. As used in line 33 of passage 2, *adamant* means
   A. a hungry animal in water.
   B. an inflexible quality.
   C. a choleric person.
   D. a source of attraction.
   E. a lack of understanding.

8. Which of the following quotes from passage 2 is in direct conflict with the ideology of passage 1?
   A. "TRAVEL, in the younger sort, is a part of education..." (line 1)
   B. "It is a strange thing, that in sea voyages, where there is nothing to be seen but sky and sea, men should make diaries..." (lines 8-9)
   C. "Let diaries therefore be brought in use." (line 11)
   D. "As for triumphs, masks, feasts, weddings...men need not be put in mind of them..." (lines 23-24)
   E. "For quarrels, they are with care and discretion to be avoided." (lines 43-44)

9. Which choice best describes the authors' preferences in travel destinations?
   A. The author of passage 2 prefers traveling to centers of culture abroad, while the author of passage 1 prefers to avoid the public.
   B. The author of passage 1 prefers nature to civilization, while the author of passage 2 appreciates manmade buildings and objects.
   C. The author of passage 1 has a deep desire to travel abroad.
   D. The author of passage 2 would probably sleep comfortably in a tent.
   E. The author of passage 2 has a greater sense of social propriety than the author of passage 1.

10. The authors of the passages would agree that
    A. it is important to designate a travel destination.
    B. people should maintain journals wherever they go.
    C. cities and monuments are the best destinations for travelers.
    D. some form of travel in one's life is important.
    E. no one needs a guide to enjoy a trip.

Lesson Thirteen

1. **implicate** (im´ pli kāt) *v.* to involve or connect unfavorably
Jeff *implicated* his friend in the crime by hiding in the friend's basement.
syn: entangle; incriminate   *ant: extricate; dissociate*

2. **analgesic** (an əl jē´ zik) *n.* a medication to reduce or eliminate pain
I took an *analgesic* to relieve my headache.
syn: painkiller   *ant: irritant*

3. **turpitude** (tûr´ pi tōōd) *n.* wickedness; vileness
In the lawless frontier town, newcomers were often shocked by the
turpitude of the residents and patrons.
syn: depravity; wantonness; decadence   *ant: purity; goodness*

4. **discretionary** (di skresh´ ə ner ē) *adj.* left to one's own judgment
Part of the grant included funds to be used specifically for research, but
the remainder of the funds were for *discretionary* use.
syn: elective; nonobligatory; unrestricted   *ant: mandatory; obligatory*

5. **flummox** (flum´ əks) *v.* to confuse; to perplex
The student's profound question *flummoxed* both the professor and the
class.
syn: bewilder; baffle; perplex   *ant: clarify; simplify*

6. **unpalatable** (un pal´ ə tə bəl) *adj.* unpleasant to the taste or the mind
The movie director deleted a scene that he thought would be *unpalatable*
to certain audiences.
syn: displeasing; objectionable; offensive   *ant: pleasing; agreeable*

7. **histrionics** (his trē on´ iks) *n.* exaggerated emotional behavior
Jane was prepared for her parents' *histrionics* when she announced her
engagement to a man they detested.
syn: theatrics; dramatics; hysterics

8. **draconian** (drā kō´ nē ən) *adj.* extremely harsh; very severe
The *draconian* rules and punishments at the prison are intended to
prevent violence.
syn: callous; merciless   *ant: lenient*

9. **noisome** (noi´ səm) *adj.* disgusting; offensive to the senses
Despite its *noisome* odor, the imported cheese is supposedly very tasty.
syn: nauseating; fetid   *ant: delightful; pleasing*

10. **punctilious** (pənk til´ ē əs) *adj.* attentive to details in conduct or action
The *punctilious* reader frequently contacted publishers to point out typographical errors in books.
syn: conscientious; particular; meticulous   *ant: careless; inattentive*

11. **veritable** (ver´ i tə bəl) *adj.* authentic; genuine
The apple tree was a *veritable* feast for the hungry deer.
syn: indubitable; bona fide   *ant: bogus; counterfeit*

12. **florid** (flôr´ id) *adj.* rosy or red in color
His face turned a *florid* shade when he became angry.
syn: ruddy; reddish; flushed

13. **fractious** (frak´ shəs) *adj.* unruly; disruptive
The *fractious* man always had something to complain about during town meetings.
syn: stubborn; difficult   *ant: temperate*

14. **moribund** (môr´ ə bund) *adj.* near death; about to die
The *moribund* patient asked his niece to come closer to hear his last request.
syn: dying; perishing   *ant: thriving; flourishing*

15. **conflagration** (kon flə grā´ shən) *n.* a large, destructive fire
The *conflagration* that began with a scented candle reduced the entire city block to ashes.
syn: blaze; inferno

EXERCISE I—Words in Context

From the list below, supply the words needed to complete the paragraph. Some words will not be used.

veritable	implicate	histrionics	unpalatable
florid	punctilious	turpitude	

1. Two consecutive nights of Shakespearean theater was a[n] _____ prize for Winona, who prefers the realism of classical actors to the _____ of most television actors. _____ members of the audience, such as Winona, noticed that good actors can even make their faces turn _____ with rage or great sadness. Winona often wonders if actors rely upon _____, personal memories to fuel the emotions they portray on the stage.

From the list below, supply the words needed to complete the paragraph. Some words will not be used.

veritable	discretionary	moribund	draconian
analgesic	flummox	noisome	

2. Randy's decision to go camping was entirely _____, but after the experience, he knew that he wouldn't be returning to the great outdoors again in the near future. On the first day, a bee stung him near his eye and caused it to swell shut. That night, as he applied a topical _____ to reduce the pain of the sting, he was overwhelmed by the _____ odor of a skunk—a skunk in his tent.

   Once he'd taken an emergency bath in the river, after being sprayed by the skunk, Randy helped his family pack up the car and leave, three days early. Randy's bad luck on the trip _____ him; he had never had such a miserable time in the wilderness. He thought that the trip might renew his _____ sense of adventure after working eight years in an office cubicle as a computer network administrator, but instead it caused him to think of how great it would be to go home to a clean shower, relax on the sofa, and maybe watch a movie in his skunk- and insect-free living room.

From the list below, supply the words needed to complete the paragraph. Some words will not be used.

implicate	florid	conflagration	fractious
turpitude	draconian	discretionary	

3.   Police suspected arson as the cause of the _____ that destroyed the apartment building, and they were thankful that the criminal's _____ had not killed anyone. A massive investigation quickly produced several suspects in the case, one of whom was _____ in the crime by mysterious burns on his hands, as though he had been too close to open flames. When the name of the suspect leaked to the general public, police had to restrain a[n] _____ mob from destroying his house in an attempt to bestow some sort of _____ justice on the man.

EXERCISE II—Sentence Completion

Complete the sentence in a way that shows you understand the meaning of the italicized vocabulary word.

1.   The previously calm peace talks turned into a *veritable* shouting match when…

2.   You can inadvertently start a *conflagration* if you…

3.   The boss assumed full responsibility for the mistake even though he could have *implicated*…

4.   Jokingly, the identical twins sometimes *flummoxed* their parents by…

5.   Few people were capable of surviving the *draconian* conditions of…

6.   Jason winced at the *noisome* sight of…

7.   The wine had a deep, *florid* color resembling that of…

8.   The teacher asked the angry drama student to save her *histrionics* for…

9.   The *fractious* patrons of the tavern near the wharf were known to…

10. The school will provide sports equipment, but players have the *discretionary* option to…

11. The doctor prescribed an *analgesic* to...

12. The *punctilious* artist was famous for his tiny...

13. Some say that publishing books on paper is a *moribund* practice because digital texts will...

14. "This is *unpalatable*," gasped the chef after...

15. The *turpitude* of a few elected officials has the potential to...

EXERCISE III—Roots, Prefixes, and Suffixes

Study the entries and answer the questions that follow.

The root *hib* means "have" or "hold."
The roots *cept* and *capt* mean "to take" or "to seize."
The prefix *in* means "in."
The prefix *ex* means "out."
The prefix *de* means "away from."
The prefix *pre* means "before."
The prefix *re* means "back" or "again."
The prefix *con* means "together."

1. Using literal translations as guidance, define the following words without using a dictionary.

   A. except   D. deception
   B. inhibit   E. exhibition
   C. precept   F. reception

2. What word comes from the *hib* root and means "to forbid"?

3. If you _____ someone's mail, then you seize it before that person receives it; however, it is illegal to take someone's mail, so the police might attempt to _____ you and put you in jail.

4. After you pay a bill, you might *take back* a document that proves that you paid. This document is called a[n] _____.

5. List as many words as you can think of that contain the prefix *pre*.

EXERCISE IV—Inference

Complete the sentences by inferring information about the italicized word from its context.

1. The Joneses knew that their son needed discipline, but they were afraid that the *draconian* rules at the military academy would...

2. If the concert crowd becomes *fractious*, the police might...

3. Some people believe that wearing helmets on motorcycles should be *discretionary* for riders, but others believe that...

EXERCISE V—Writing

Here is a writing prompt similar to the one you will find on the writing portion of the SAT.

Plan and write an essay based on the following statement:

> The superior man understands what is right; the inferior man understands what will sell.
> —Confucius (551–479 B.C.)

Assignment: The Chinese philosopher Confucius was said to have knowledge beyond the ages. In an essay, explain the meaning of the quotation and how it might apply to a modern situation or person. Support your essay using evidence from your reading, studies, or observations and experience.

Thesis: Write a one-sentence response to the above assignment. Make certain this sentence offers a clear statement of your position.

Example: Though Confucius lived long before modern philosophies involving enterprise and entrepreneurship, he knew that financial success has little bearing on moral or spiritual status.

Organizational Plan: If your thesis is the point on which you want to end, where does your essay need to begin? List the points of development that are inevitable in leading your reader from your beginning point to your end point. This list is your outline.

Draft: Use your thesis as both your beginning and your end. Following your outline, write a good first draft of your essay. Remember to support all of your points with examples, facts, references to reading, etc.

Review and revise: Exchange essays with a classmate. Using the scoring guide for Development on page 249, score your partner's essay (while he or she scores yours). Focus on the development of ideas and the use of language conventions. If necessary, rewrite your essay to improve the development of ideas and your use of language.

Identifying Sentence Errors

Identify the grammatical error in each of the following sentences. If the sentence contains no error, select answer E.

1. Many students <u>look much</u> different <u>than</u> they did last <u>semester;</u>
            (A)   (B)   (C)
    <u>it's</u> probably because of <u>their new outfits.</u>   <u>No error</u>
                      (D)   (E)

2. Both my <u>brother-in-laws</u> <u>work</u> at the same <u>company, and</u> they are trying
              (A)   (B)   (C)
    to get me <u>an interview</u> for a job there.   <u>No error</u>
              (D)   (E)

3. <u>Would you please</u> tell the delivery <u>person to sit</u> the packages on the
       (A)   (B)
    <u>kitchen table?</u> <u>I'll pay him after I find my purse.</u>   <u>No error</u>
        (C)   (D)   (E)

4. <u>All members of the volunteer fire company</u>, and even their dog,
        (A)
    <u>received a</u> commendation from the mayor for <u>its enormous</u> efforts
       (B)   (C)
    during the <u>fund-raising drive.</u>   <u>No error</u>
            (D)   (E)

5. If I <u>had brought</u> enough money, I definitely <u>would have purchased</u> the car
        (A)   (B)
    I wanted at last <u>week's auction</u> in <u>Marvell, New York.</u>   <u>No error</u>
            (C)   (D)   (E)

Improving Sentences

The underlined portion of each sentence below contains some flaw. Select the answer that best corrects the flaw.

6. If you will pay close attention to what I actually say, <u>you will be able to understand my instructions more perfectly.</u>
   A. you might be able to understand my instructions more perfectly.
   B. it will be an easy time understanding my instructions.
   C. you will understand my instructions perfectly and ably.
   D. you will be able to understand my instructions perfectly.
   E. my instructions will be able to be understood by you perfectly.

7. <u>My father objects to me playing football because of the dangers</u> inherent in any contact sport.
   A. My father objects to my playing football because of the dangers
   B. My father objects to playing football because of the dangers
   C. My father objects to me playing because of the dangers in football, which are
   D. Because of the dangers, my father objects to me playing football
   E. My father objects to football because of the dangers

8. Most of the mowing of our lawn was done <u>by the two oldest of the three sons, my brother and I.</u>
   A. by two of the three sons, my brother and I.
   B. by the two eldest of the three sons, my brother and me.
   C. by the two elders of the three sons, my brother and I.
   D. by my brother and I, the two oldest of the three sons,
   E. by the oldest of the three sons, my brother and I.

9. <u>The United States, as the worlds preeminent democracy, must always protect the right's of their citizens.</u>
   A. The United States, as the world's pre-eminent Democracy, must always protect the right's of their citizens.
   B. The United States is the worlds' preeminent democracy, and must always protect the rights of their citizens.
   C. The United States, as the world's preeminent democracy, must always protect the right's of it's citizens.
   D. The United States, as the worlds preeminent democracy, must always protect it's citizen's right's.
   E. The United States, as the world's preeminent democracy, must always protect the rights of its citizens.

10. The physician says that <u>there is always the possibility that the cancer might return, but so far, there has been no signs of a recurrence.</u>
   A.   there was always the possibility that the cancer might return, but so far, there has been no signs of a recurrence.
   B.   there is always the possibilities that the cancer might return, but so far, there has been no signs of any recurrence.
   C.   there is always the possibility that the cancer might return, but so far, there was no signs of a recurrence.
   D.   there is always the possibility that the cancer might return, but so far, there have been no signs of a recurrence.
   E.   there always is the possibility that the cancer might return, but so far there has been not any sign of it recurring.

Lesson Fourteen

1. **protégé** (prō´ tə zhā) *n.* a person under the guidance or training of another
   When the famous artist died, his young *protégé* began a long and successful career.
   syn: apprentice   *ant: mentor*

2. **indiscernible** (in di sûr´ nə bəl) *adj.* difficult or impossible to discern or perceive
   The flaw in the paint was *indiscernible* unless you knew where to look.
   syn: imperceptible; indistinguishable; subtle   *ant: evident; noticeable; obvious*

3. **virulent** (vir´ yə lənt) *adj.* extremely infectious or poisonous
   The hospital used an incinerator to destroy any *virulent* waste.
   syn: venomous; toxic   *ant: harmless*

4. **phlegmatic** (fleg mat´ ik) *adj.* calm and unemotional
   The *phlegmatic* man didn't even smile when he saw that he had a winning lottery ticket.
   syn: apathetic; cold; unfeeling   *ant: lively; excited*

5. **artisan** (är´ ti zən) *n.* a skilled manual worker; a craftsperson
   Mike hired *artisans* from the welder's union to make repairs to the steel holding tanks.

6. **reciprocate** (ri sip´ rə kāt) *v.* to give in response to receiving something
   The teacher explained that he would *reciprocate* good classroom behavior by grading on a curve.
   syn: match

7. **tenable** (ten´ ə bəl) *adj.* rationally defensible
   After hearing the defendant's *tenable* reason for stealing the car, the jury found him not guilty.
   syn: sound; viable; credible   *ant: questionable; unbelievable*

8. **boondoggle** (bōōn´ dôg əl) *n.* an unnecessary, wasteful project
   Some people believe that building a space station is a *boondoggle* because any resulting advancements will not offset the cost of construction.

9. **curmudgeon** (kər muj´ ən) *n.* a stubborn, ill-tempered person
The old *curmudgeon* sat on the bench at the mall and complained to anyone who would listen.
syn: grouch; bellyacher; killjoy

10. **moiety** (moi´ ə tē) *n.* a portion or part of something
Each of the heirs received a *moiety* of his uncle's large estate.
syn: division; piece

11. **inculcate** (in kəl´ kāt) *v.* to impress upon or teach someone by repetition
The chemistry teacher *inculcated* atomic mass values into her students until they could recite the numbers without looking at a chart.

12. **fiduciary** (fə dōō´ shē er ē) *adj.* relating to the governing of property or estate on behalf of others
Mr. Montaire has the *fiduciary* duty of controlling the family fortune until his nephew turns eighteen.

13. **repugnant** (ri pug´ nənt) *adj.* offensive; repulsive
The *repugnant* comedian depended on shock, not talent, to make a living.
syn: abhorrent; obnoxious   *ant: appealing; enjoyable; nice*

14. **opprobrium** (ə prō´ brē əm) *n.* disgrace; extreme dishonor
The vandals who desecrated the church were regarded with *opprobrium* in the years following the crime.
syn: obloquy; ignominy; shame   *ant: esteem; honor; respect*

15. **potentate** (pōt´ n tāt) *n.* a monarch; one who has great power
Diamond Jim, a real estate *potentate*, is said to own half of the state.
syn: sovereign; magnate; king   *ant: peasant; plebian; serf*

EXERCISE I—Words in Context

From the list below, supply the words needed to complete the paragraph. Some words will not be used.

virulent	artisan	protégé	reciprocate
inculcate	fiduciary	indiscernible	

1. To some, Kurt was a simple stonemason who built fireplaces or walls next to driveways, but James, Kurt's young _____, recognized that the aging man was a[n] _____ who worked with natural stones as an artist would work with paint. James had been Kurt's assistant for several years, and during that time, Kurt _____ the many tricks and techniques for creating impressive masonry. In time, James was able to stack and chisel stones and make the natural flaws _____, just as Kurt had done for nearly fifty years. Before Kurt passed away, he gave James _____ responsibility of the business, pleased that the ancient craft would last for another generation.

From the list below, supply the words needed to complete the paragraph. Some words will not be used.

repugnant	protégé	reciprocate	boondoggle
phlegmatic	tenable	curmudgeon	

2. Agnes scolded her husband of fifty years for being such a[n] _____.

    "Your constant griping is _____; it's no wonder no one wants to visit any more. Unlike your grumpy friends, our grandchildren don't care to _____ your incessant complaining with complaints of their own. Yes, dear, you make some _____ arguments, but sometimes you need to be more optimistic." Harold, briefly _____ and unresponsive, exhaled in antipathy and continued to watch a rerun of his favorite television game show. He had to catch himself before yelling at the contestant who he knew would lose the big prize at the end.

From the list below, supply the words needed to complete the paragraph. Some words will not be used.

curmudgeon   virulent   boondoggle   moiety
potentate   tenable   opprobrium

3.   P.J. Tucker, the _____ at the helm of the twelfth-largest corporation on Earth, squinted when he saw the company's fiscal data for the quarter. A recent series of acquisitions had turned into a[n] _____, because two of the newly acquired companies had failed miserably. P.J. knew that if news of the loss got out, the _____ rumor would spread through the corporation like a disease. Workers, each of whom had contributed a[n] _____ of his or her life to the success of the company, would now be forced to endure widespread cutbacks and layoffs. P.J. knew that thousands of his employees would view him with _____ for years as the wealthy executive who fired thousands of workers to protect his own fortune.

EXERCISE II—Sentence Completion

Complete the sentence in a way that shows you understand the meaning of the italicized vocabulary word.

1. Jerry, the spatula *potentate* of the kitchen utensil industry, had contracts with…

2. During construction of the mansion, woodworking *artisans* were hired to…

3. Kim felt that she deserved at least a *moiety* of credit for the team's championship season because…

4. The scientist's young *protégé* quickly learned…

5. When George refused to curb his *repugnant* language at work, the supervisor…

6. Half of Congress felt that the nation had a *tenable* reason for going to war, but the other half…

7. The piano teacher *inculcated* the major musical scales into her students by…

8. The Center for Disease Control quarantined the person with a *virulent* strain of Anthrax before the disease…

9. Constructing a new warehouse while sales were floundering proved to be a *boondoggle* that caused…

10. Mortimer has *fiduciary* responsibility for the charitable organization, so he decides…

11. The *curmudgeon* frequently wrote letters to the editor of the newspaper demanding…

12. During the hurricane, the *phlegmatic* ship captain showed little…

13. When his neighbor shovels snow from Joe's sidewalk, Joe *reciprocates* by…

14. The *indiscernible* stain on the carpet is noticeable only if you…

15. Though the man was found innocent in court, he lived in *opprobrium* for years because…

EXERCISE III—Roots, Prefixes, and Suffixes

Study the entries and answer the questions that follow.

The root *pugn* means "fight."
The root *bell* means "war."
The root *pac* means "peace."
The suffix *ious* means "full of."
The suffix *ose* means "full of."
The prefix *re* means "back" or "again."
The prefix *ante* means "before."

1. Using literal translations as guidance, define the following words without using a dictionary.

    A. repugnant   D. antebellum
    B. pacify   E. pugnacious
    C. belligerent   F. pact

2. The prefix *im* means "against," so what do you think it means to *impugn* someone's claim?

3. How do you think the Pacific Ocean got its name?

4. Someone who fights back against the rules might be called a[n] _____.

5. List as many words as you can think of that contain the root *pac*.

EXERCISE IV—Inference

Complete the sentences by inferring information about the italicized word from its context.

1. Someone who has a *virulent* cold should not...

2. Customers complained about Jake's *repugnant* behavior at the upscale restaurant when he...

3. If you fail to *reciprocate* when someone treats you well, then that person...

EXERCISE V—Critical Reading

Below is a reading passage followed by several multiple-choice questions similar to the ones you will encounter on the SAT. Carefully read the passage and choose the best answer to each of the questions.

Joseph Conrad wrote the classic novella, "Heart of Darkness," in 1899, during the peak of the British Empire. In the story, Marlow, a steamboat captain and narrator of the tale, recounts his voyage deep into the Congo, which was a Belgian territory at the time. Marlow has the mission of contacting Kurtz, an ivory trader who works for the Belgian company deep in the Congo at the "inner station." The following excerpt from "Heart of Darkness" begins with Marlow's arrival at a Belgian station thirty miles from the mouth of the Congo.

"There's your company's station," said the Swede, pointing to three wooden barrack-like structures on the rocky slope. "I will send your things up. Four boxes did you say? So. Farewell."

    I came upon a boiler wallowing in the grass, then found a path leading up the
5 hill. It turned aside for the boulders, and also for an undersized railway truck lying there on its back with its wheels in the air. One was off. The thing looked as dead as the carcass of some animal. I came upon more pieces of decaying machinery, a stack of rusty rails. To the left a clump of trees made a shady spot, where dark things seemed to stir feebly. I blinked, the path was steep. A horn tooted to the
10 right, and I saw the black people run. A heavy and dull detonation shook the ground, a puff of smoke came out of the cliff, and that was all. No change appeared on the face of the rock. They were building a railway. The cliff was not in the way or anything; but this objectless blasting was all the work going on.

    A slight clinking behind me made me turn my head. Six black men advanced in
15 a file, toiling up the path. They walked erect and slow, balancing small baskets full of earth on their heads, and the clink kept time with their footsteps. Black rags were wound round their loins, and the short ends behind waggled to and fro like tails. I could see every rib, the joints of their limbs were like knots in a rope; each had an iron collar on his neck, and all were connected together with a chain whose bights
20 swung between them, rhythmically clinking. Another report from the cliff made me think suddenly of that ship of war I had seen firing into a continent. It was the same kind of ominous voice; but these men could by no stretch of imagination be called enemies. They were called criminals, and the outraged law, like the bursting shells, had come to them, an insoluble mystery from the sea. All their meager breasts
25 panted together, the violently dilated nostrils quivered, the eyes stared stonily uphill. They passed me within six inches, without a glance, with that complete, death-like indifference of unhappy savages. Behind this raw matter one of the reclaimed, the product of the new forces at work, strolled despondently, carrying a rifle by its middle. He had a uniform jacket with one button off, and seeing a white
30 man on the path, hoisted his weapon to his shoulder with alacrity. This was simple prudence, white men being so much alike at a distance that he could not tell who

I might be. He was speedily reassured, and with a large, white, rascally grin, and a glance at his charge, seemed to take me into partnership in his exalted trust. After all, I also was a part of the great cause of these high and just proceedings.

35   Instead of going up, I turned and descended to the left. My idea was to let that chain gang get out of sight before I climbed the hill. You know I am not particularly tender; I've had to strike and to fend off. I've had to resist and to attack sometimes—that's only one way of resisting—without counting the exact cost, according to the demands of such sort of life as I had blundered into. I've seen the devil

40   of violence, and the devil of greed, and the devil of hot desire; but, by all the stars! these were strong, lusty, red-eyed devils, that swayed and drove men—men, I tell you. But as I stood on this hillside, I foresaw that in the blinding sunshine of that land I would become acquainted with a flabby, pretending, weak-eyed devil of a rapacious and pitiless folly. How insidious he could be, too, I was only to find out

45   several months later and a thousand miles farther. For a moment I stood appalled, as though by a warning. Finally I descended the hill, obliquely, towards the tree I had seen.

I avoided a vast artificial hole somebody had been digging on the slope, the purpose of which I found it impossible to divine. It wasn't a quarry or a sandpit, any-

50   how. It was just a hole. It might have been connected with the philanthropic desire of giving the criminals something to do. I don't know. Then I nearly fell into a very narrow ravine, almost no more than a scar in the hillside. I discovered that a lot of imported drainage pipes for the settlement had been tumbled in there. There wasn't one that was not broken. It was a wanton smashup. At last I got under the trees.

55   My purpose was to stroll into the shade for a moment; but no sooner within than it seemed to me I had stepped into the gloomy circle of some inferno. The rapids were near, and an uninterrupted, uniform, headlong, rushing noise filled the mournful stillness of the grove, where not a breath stirred, not a leaf moved, with a mysterious sound—as though the tearing pace of the launched earth had sud-

60   denly become audible.

Black shapes crouched, lay, sat between the trees leaning against the trunks, clinging to the earth, half coming out, half effaced within the dim light, in all the attitudes of pain, abandonment, and despair. Another mine on the cliff went off, followed by a slight shudder of the soil under my feet. The work was going on. The

65   work! And this was the place where some of the helpers had withdrawn to die.

They were dying slowly—it was very clear. They were not enemies, they were not criminals, they were nothing earthly now, nothing but black shadows of disease and starvation, lying confusedly in the greenish gloom. Brought from all the recesses of the coast in all the legality of time contracts, lost in uncongenial surroundings, fed

70   on unfamiliar food, they sickened, became inefficient, and were then allowed to crawl away and rest. These moribund shapes were free as air—and nearly as thin. I began to distinguish the gleam of the eyes under the trees. Then, glancing down, I saw a face near my hand. The black bones reclined at full length with one shoulder against the tree, and slowly the eyelids rose and the sunken eyes looked up at

75   me, enormous and vacant, a kind of blind, white flicker in the depths of the orbs, which died out slowly. The man seemed young—almost a boy—but you know with them it's hard to tell. I found nothing else to do but to offer him one of my good Swede's ship's biscuits I had in my pocket. The fingers closed slowly on it and held—there was no other movement and no other glance. He had tied a bit of white

80   worsted round his neck—Why? Where did he get it? Was it a badge—an orna-
ment—a charm—a propitiatory act? Was there any idea at all connected with it? It
looked startling round his black neck, this bit of white thread from beyond the seas.

1. As used in line 20, *report* most nearly means
    A. account.
    B. breeze.
    C. inform.
    D. shot.
    E. test.

2. The narrator of the passage is probably
    A. one of the enslaved workers.
    B. a white newcomer to the station.
    C. an official of the colony that he is describing.
    D. a high-ranking native worker for the station.
    E. the Swedish captain.

3. Which choice best describes the author's purpose for including the following line?

      "After all, I also was a part of the great cause of these high and just
      proceedings."

    A. He is demonstrating his own nationalism.
    B. He is suggesting his relief that the colony is now civilized.
    C. He is sarcastically criticizing the jurisprudence of the colonies.
    D. He is mocking the prisoners.
    E. He is boasting about his high status in the Congo.

4. As used in line 41, *swayed* most nearly means
    A. spoke to.
    B. governed.
    C. timed.
    D. staggered.
    E. hired.

5. To whom or what does the following quotation refer?

   "...flabby, pretending, weak-eyed devil of a rapacious and pitiless folly"
   (lines 43-44)

   A. to Marlow, the narrator
   B. to the criminals blasting rock from the cliff face
   C. to the Belgians controlling the territory
   D. to a person the narrator eventually meets
   E. to the man guarding the chain gang

6. In his use of physical description, the author of the passage suggests that eyes
   A. are often symbolic in literature.
   B. reflect man's inner nature.
   C. are unimportant to laborers.
   D. reveal one's sins.
   E. require special care in the jungle.

7. As used in line 49, *divine* most nearly means
   A. mistake.
   B. neat.
   C. orderly.
   D. discover.
   E. celestial.

8. According to the passage, what characteristic does the blasting of the cliff share with the hole on the slope in paragraph 5?
   A. Both of the projects appear to be entirely unnecessary.
   B. Both of the projects were supervised by the narrator.
   C. Colonists provide the labor for both projects.
   D. The prisoners probably dug the hole.
   E. Both the hole and the cliff are symbols of government.

9. In the final paragraph, the narrator declares that the people beneath the trees are not criminals because
   A. they did not have proper trials.
   B. they are political enemies, not criminals.
   C. most of them are from other nations.
   D. the narrator recognizes one of them, and he is not a criminal.
   E. they do not even appear to be human.

10. According to the passage, which word best describes the narrator's feelings about the scenes he witnesses?
    A. fear
    B. indifference
    C. pride
    D. horror
    E. disruption

REVIEW

Lessons 8 – 14

EXERCISE I – Sentence Completion

Choose the best pair of words to complete the sentence. Most choices will fit grammatically and will even make sense logically, but you must choose the pair that best fits the idea of the sentence.

Note that these words are not taken directly from lessons in this book. This exercise is intended to replicate the sentence completion portion of the SAT.

1. During her long hike along the Appalachian Trail, Lea carried a heavy, _____ backpack, and she _____ many animals she had never seen before.
    A. leather, spied
    B. cumbersome, encountered
    C. full, estimated
    D. necessary, photographed
    E. rainproof, frightened

2. The humorous discussion about politics between the two friends suddenly _____ into a[n] _____, so they agreed that the subject must never come up again.
    A. elevated, fistfight
    B. turned, agreement
    C. swirled, disagreement
    D. escalated, argument
    E. energized, fight

3. "If you insist on _____ my criminal record," said the mayor to his opponent, "I will certainly not _____ to bring up your arrest for tax evasion."
    A. demeaning, dare
    B. avoiding, quibble
    C. mentioning, desire
    D. distorting, hesitate
    E. destroying, regret

4. Despite the _____ king's having ruled his country _____, the majority of people still respected him; however, a growing number began to think of him as evil.
   A. elderly, kindly
   B. gregarious, benevolently
   C. despotic, cruelly
   D. angry, dictatorially
   E. fierce, arrogantly

5. Jack, the one person in the office on whom the boss could _____, was unfortunately away from his desk when his assistance was

   _____.
   A. depend, paramount
   B. rely, effective
   C. count, satisfactory
   D. lean, beneficial
   E. implore, crucial

6. "The _____ of author Ernest Hemingway," said the _____, "is not as accurate when he deals with women as when writing about men."
   A. perceptiveness, critic
   B. responses, teacher
   C. outlook, writer
   D. quality, essayist
   E. portrayal, biographer

7. _____ from the failed experiment caused the cancer cells to _____ rapidly.
   A. Mistakes, explode
   B. Flaws, die
   C. Corruption, multiply
   D. Protoplasm, increase
   E. Radiation, mutate

8. To be in _____ with the new regulations, construction companies must submit their up-to-date _____ by next week.
   A. agreement, notification
   B. actuality, agreements
   C. non-compliance, alterations
   D. compliance, revisions
   E. competition, blueprints

EXERCISE II – Crossword Puzzle

Use the clues to complete the crossword puzzle. The answers consist of vocabulary words from lessons 8 through 14.

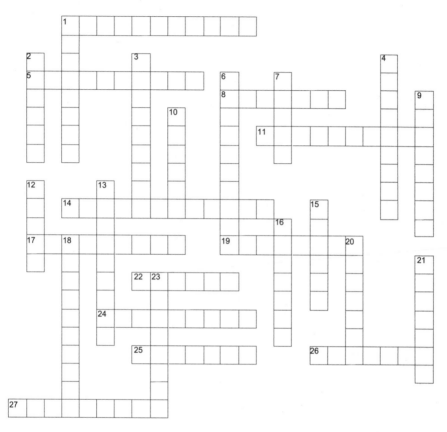

Across
1. uneasiness caused by guilt
5. disgrace; dishonor
8. to protest
11. a tip
14. insincere; calculating
17. to connect unfavorably
19. error in speech or manners
22. beneficial
24. impossible to defend
25. rationally defensible
26. childish
27. unruly; disruptive

Down
1. deserving blame
2. a portion or part
3. extremely harsh
4. wickedness
6. indirect; roundabout
7. to take pleasure in
9. wildly excited
10. useless; futile
12. indicated but not expressed
13. diligent; persistent
15. carefree
16. relating to ordinary people
18. calm and unemotional
20. vague bodily discomfort
21. a cure-all
23. an explanation of a text

Lesson Fifteen

1. **prominent** (prom´ ə nənt) *adj.* very noticeable or obvious
   The trunk is a *prominent* feature of an elephant.
   syn: conspicuous; clear   *ant: inconspicuous*

2. **autonomy** (ô ton´ ə mē) *n.* independence
   Vicky enjoys the *autonomy* of being self-employed as a freelance writer.
   syn: self-rule; license; sovereignty   *ant: subordination*

3. **gustatory** (gus´ tə tôr ē) *adj.* relating to the sense of taste
   The gourmet dinner lacked the *gustatory* appeal that Julie expected.

4. **chthonian** (thō´ nē ən) *adj.* pertaining to the underworld; dwelling in
   or beneath the surface of the earth
   The *chthonian* engraving in the tomb featured a lion guarding the gates of
   the netherworld.

5. **extirpate** (ek´ stər pāt) *v.* to root out or eradicate; to destroy
   completely
   New weeds sprouted faster than Bob could *extirpate* them.
   syn: expunge; uproot; exterminate   *ant: generate; propagate*

6. **coagulate** (kō ag´ yə lāt) *v.* to change or be changed from liquid into
   a thickened or solid mass
   You should clean the spilled cooking grease before it *coagulates* on the
   floor.
   syn: congeal; solidify; curdle   *ant: liquefy*

7. **puissance** (pwē´ səns) *n.* power; might
   You'll need considerable *puissance* to win the game tomorrow, so get
   plenty of rest.
   syn: strength; vigor   *ant: frailty; weakness*

8. **appellation** (ap ə lā´ shən) *n.* name, title, or designation
   The pre-med student hoped to earn the *appellation* of "Doctor."
   syn: denomination; classification

9. **peripatetic** (per ə pə te´ tik) *adj.* traveling, especially by foot
   The *peripatetic* wanderer seldom passed through the same town twice.
   syn: ambulant; vagabond; nomadic   *ant: stationary*

10. **misanthrope** (mis´ ən thrōp) *n.* one who hates or mistrusts
humankind
The *misanthrope* never travels far from his remote cabin, and he threatens
anyone who wanders near it.
ant: samaritan

11. **tutelary** (tōōt´ ə ler ē) *adj.* pertaining to guardianship
Donald had enough *tutelary* experience to be a good foster father.
syn: custodial; guardian

12. **scion** (sī´ ən) *n.* descendant; heir
The *scions* of the wealthy industrialist quickly squandered the family
fortune.
syn: successor; progeny   *ant: predecessor; ancestor*

13. **jurisprudence** (jŏŏr is prōōd´ ns) *n.* the science, philosophy, and
application of the law
The judge had to dismiss the case because of the prosecutor's faulty
jurisprudence.

14. **supercilious** (sōō pər sil´ ē əs) *adj.* contemptuous; arrogant
The *supercilious* widow raised her eyebrows and looked away when I
greeted her.
syn: haughty; condescending; conceited   *ant: modest; humble*

15. **malevolent** (mə lev´ ə lənt) *adj.* having ill-will; wishing harm; evil
The burglar turned and ran when he met the *malevolent* stare of a large
guard dog.
syn: malicious; sinister; menacing   *ant: benevolent*

EXERCISE I—Words in Context

*From the list below, supply the words needed to complete the paragraph. Some
words will not be used.*

gustatory	extirpate	autonomy	misanthrope
peripatetic	malevolent	chthonian	

1.   The old _____, convinced that everyone he met had _____
intentions meant to harm him, relocated his home to a remote mountain
cabin, far from the civilization he loathed. With the exception of his tools,

clothing, rifle, and ammunition, he _____ every possible trace of the outside world from his cabin. Other than his _____ foraging in the wilderness for food or firewood, the hermit never again left the valley or visited the small town eight miles south of the cabin. In a short time, the hermit's _____ preferences changed from those of average, domestic meals to the tastes of nuts, berries, and wild game.

From the list below, supply the words needed to complete the paragraph. Some words will not be used.

puissance	scion	misanthrope	prominent
autonomy	supercilious	appellation	

2. After three years of working at the department store, Mark was the _____ candidate for the promotion to manager. He eagerly anticipated the _____ that accompanied the position; there would be no more punch clocks and time cards, and no more _____ boss to belittle or second-guess Mark's decisions. Mark was certain that he had the _____ to work his way to the top of the company and eventually become a[n] _____ of the corporate dynasty.

From the list below, supply the words needed to complete the paragraph. Some words will not be used.

peripatetic	chthonian	puissance	coagulate
tutelary	jurisprudence	appellation	

3. Audrey looked at an old photograph of her grandfather when he was a coal miner. Blackened with coal dust and squinting at the sun, grandfather looked like a[n] _____ creature emerging from his subterranean lair. Audrey, who knew her grandfather by the _____ "Papa," missed the wise old man's _____ guidance. Before Audrey enrolled in law school, she and her grandfather had often discussed the way in which _____ had changed from one generation to the next. In the days following the funeral, Audrey's fond memories seemed to _____ into a lump of sadness that weighed heavy in her being.

EXERCISE II—Sentence Completion

Complete the sentence in a way that shows you understand the meaning of the italicized vocabulary word.

1. The *supercilious* waiter didn't want to serve us because...

2. Gina thought that her neighbor was some kind of *misanthrope* because he...

3. It took weeks for Wendy to learn everyone's proper *appellation* after she accepted a job at...

4. When experiencing their first taste of *autonomy*, many young adults...

5. Millionaires with humble beginnings resented the *scions* of the railroad magnate because they...

6. During a secret meeting in the underground headquarters, the evil genius outlined his *malevolent* plan to...

7. The hot candle wax will *coagulate* when...

8. Donald developed a *tutelary* relationship with his niece because...

9. Jane braved the snowstorm, but she didn't know if she would have the *puissance* to...

10. American *jurisprudence* disallows a person to be permanently imprisoned without...

11. The ancient Greeks carved a *chthonian* deity into the prow of their warship in order to...

12. The explorer was surprised to find that the *gustatory* preferences of the natives were...

13. The dictator attempted to *extirpate* any dissidents from the ranks of his army by...

14. The witness easily identified the criminal when she saw his *prominent*...

15. Nancy preferred *peripatetic* vacations to...

EXERCISE III—Roots, Prefixes, and Suffixes

Study the entries and answer the questions that follow.

The roots *mit* and *miss* mean "send."
The root *duct* means "to lead."
The prefix *dis* means "away."
The prefix *ad* means "toward."
The prefix *ab* means "away from."
The prefix *in* means "into."
The prefix *trans* means "across."

1. *Using literal translations as guidance, define the following words without using a dictionary.*

    A. dismiss   D. abduct
    B. remit   E. induct
    C. admit   F. transmission

2. The prefix *per* means "through," so what does the word *permit* literally mean?

3. The prefix *de* means "from." If your process of reasoning leads you to an idea, you might call that idea a[n] _____.

4. An *emissary* is someone sent out to deliver a specific message, and a lamp _____, or "sends out" light. We can assume that the *e* prefix means _____.

5. Iron and copper are good _____ because they can be used to lead electrical current from one place to another.

6. What do you think the word *missile* literally means?

7. List as many words as you can think of that contain the prefix *trans*.

EXERCISE IV—Inference

Complete the sentences by inferring information about the italicized word from its context.

1. If you underestimate the *puissance* of your enemy, you might...

2. A *misanthrope* who avoids contact with people might not appreciate it if you...

3. If you fail to *extirpate* the bamboo shoots in your lawn, the plants might...

EXERCISE V—Writing

Here is a writing prompt similar to the one you will find on the writing portion of the SAT.

Plan and write an essay based on the following statement:

> "Far better it is to dare mighty things, to win glorious triumphs, even though checkered by failure, than to take rank with those poor spirits who neither enjoy much nor suffer much, because they live in the gray twilight that knows not victory nor defeat."
>
> –Theodore Roosevelt

Assignment: Decide whether you agree or disagree with Teddy Roosevelt's suggestion that it is better to fail than it is never to have tried. In an essay, explain why Roosevelt's statement is realistic or not, and support your argument using an example from history, current events, literature, or your experience or observation.

Thesis: Write a one-sentence response to the above assignment. Make certain this single sentence offers a clear statement of your position.

Example: In his bold suggestion to dare mighty things, Roosevelt wrongly implies that it is shameful to live in timid, "gray twilight"; most people strive to lead lives without extremes because they cannot live comfortably while enduring the constant peril that "glorious triumphs" might induce.

Organizational Plan: If your thesis is the point on which you want to end, where does your essay need to begin? List the points of development that are inevitable in leading your reader from your beginning point to your end point. This list is your outline.

Draft: Use your thesis as both your beginning and your end. Following your outline, write a good first draft of your essay. Remember to support all of your points with examples, facts, references to reading, etc.

Review and revise: Exchange essays with a classmate. Using the scoring guide for Sentence Formation and Variety on page 250, score your partner's essay (while he or she scores yours). Focus on the sentence structure and the use of language conventions. If necessary, rewrite your essay to improve the sentence structure and your use of language.

Improving Paragraphs

Read the following passage and then answer the multiple-choice questions that follow. The questions will require you to make decisions regarding the revision of the reading selection.

1   The yawn—that irritating, ungainly, impolite disruption in board meetings, classrooms, and assembly lines all over the world—is but one of the great mysteries of humankind. Despite centuries of research, not one scientist can say with certainty why, exactly, people yawn. Oh, yes, they theorize; lines of physiologists spout their suppositions: "Excessive carbon dioxide in the lungs!" "Under-stimulated brains!" "A primal response to ward off predators!" Unfortunately, while it would be fantastic if a simple yawn could frighten away a saber-toothed tiger, the real reason for yawning is anyone's guess.

2   People begin expressing their boredom very early in life—even before their born. The fact that fetuses yawn tells researchers that yawning is both involuntary and not due to a general lack of oxygen, since babies in utero do not breath oxygen as adults do. Now, simply determining why babies yawn has become a part of the quest to solve the riddle of yawns. One theory that currently holds water is that yawning releases a chemical called *surfactant*, a substance that ensures that the alveoli, or tiny air pockets in the lungs, stay open. The production of surfactant is critical to development because it ensures that the lungs of a newborn will be ready to survive outside the womb; however, as everyone knows, the yawning continues well beyond birth.

3   Boring classes, office meetings, lectures, seminars, and traffic jams take quite a toll on brains, and yawning does help to revive brains to better cope with the drudgery of staying awake; however, yawning often strikes at seemingly arbitrary times. Stressful situations often beget yawns, as do colds, allergies, and sinus problems; even strenuous activity can spark excessive yawning. Experts agree that the lungs stretch during yawning, and the stretching prevents the collapse of tiny airways. This might help to explain why yawning that accompanies periods of shallow breathing, such as before and after sleeping, helps more air to enter the respiratory system. More air is good.

4   The seemingly arbitrary nature of yawning has prompted many scientists to suggest that yawning is actually a form of involuntary communication. Both human beings are creatures of imitation and quite receptive to suggestion; fifty-five percent of all people, in fact, will yawn within five minutes after seeing someone else yawn. Reading about yawns also has this effect, as well as talking about them and even thinking about them. Yawns also can express strong antisocial messages. Yawns are widely perceived as rude gestures. They frequently imply boredom, but yawns often accompany feelings of rejection or even anger. Some medical professionals claim that yawning is stimulated by the same chemicals in the brain that effect emotions, moods, and appetites, so perhaps to ancient ancestors, yawns were involuntary, visual signals that alerted people that it was time to seek shelter for the night, which therefore synchronized sleeping patterns. Humans are, after all, social beings.

5   Perhaps someday scientists will find the proper combination of theories that explains yawning once and for all. There seems to be a connection between prenatal yawns producing surfactant and adult yawns filling tiny airways in the lungs, but the ease with which humans will yawn simply because they saw someone else yawn suggests that the act is purely psychosomatic. Despite the many theories and facts pertaining to its origins, the mysterious act of yawning must join the tailbone and the appendix on the list of human anatomical conundrums.

1.   Which choice best describes an error in the first sentence of paragraph 2?
     A.   subject-pronoun disagreement
     B.   illogical relationship
     C.   mixed metaphor
     D.   incorrect possessive pronoun
     E.   double negative

2.   Which choice would improve the following sentence from paragraph 2?

         One theory that currently holds water is that yawning releases a chemical called *surfactant*, a substance that ensures that the alveoli, or tiny air pockets in the lungs, stay open.

     A.   Rewrite the sentence to omit the cliché.
     B.   Make two sentences out of the original sentence.
     C.   Use the sentence as the introduction of the paragraph.
     D.   Change *yawning* to *a yawn*.
     E.   Capitalize *alveoli*, and place a semicolon after *surfactant*.

3.   Which sentence should be deleted from paragraph 3?
     A.   sentence 1
     B.   sentence 2
     C.   sentence 3
     D.   sentence 4
     E.   sentence 5

4.   Correcting which error would fix the second sentence of paragraph 4?
     A.   semicolon use
     B.   use of *both*
     C.   the hyphen in *fifty-five*
     D.   missing linking verb
     E.   *else* not possessive

5. Which redundant sentence should be removed from paragraph 4?
    A. sentence 1
    B. sentence 2
    C. sentence 3
    D. sentence 5
    E. sentence 6

Lesson Sixteen

1. **trenchant** (tren´ chənt) *adj.* effectively keen and forceful in thought or expression
The expert's *trenchant* comments silenced his critics.
syn: cutting; forthright   *ant: ambiguous; lenient; insipid*

2. **bourgeois** (bŏŏr zhwä´) *adj.* relating to the middle class
Adam hoped to become wealthy and abandon his *bourgeois* life.

3. **nascent** (nā´ sənt) *adj.* emerging; coming into existence
Jill attributed her *nascent* interest in sailing to her discovery of her seafaring ancestors.
syn: blooming; fledgling   *ant: dying; withering*

4. **indefeasible** (in di fē´ zə bəl) *adj.* not capable of being undone or voided
When times were rough, Teresa found comfort in the *indefeasible* love of her parents.
syn: immutable; unremitting; constant   *ant: varying; irregular; temporary*

5. **paladin** (pa´ lə dən) *n.* a heroic champion or leader
Though he was nothing more than a fictional cartoon character, Captain Justice was an inspiring *paladin* to children everywhere.
          ant: villain

6. **sine qua non** (sin i kwä nän´) *n.* something essential; a prerequisite
Good communication is the *sine qua non* of a productive workplace.
syn: must; requirement; necessity   *ant: option*

7. **arcane** (är kān´) *adj.* known or understood by only a few; mysterious
The alchemist claimed to know an *arcane* formula for turning iron into gold.
syn: secret; obscure; esoteric   *ant: famous; obvious; exoteric*

8. **tangential** (tan jen´ shəl) *adj.* merely touching or slightly connected; digressing from the main point
The chairman asked the board to avoid *tangential* issues during the important meeting.
syn: nonessential; peripheral   *ant: vital; crucial; relevant*

9. **mercurial** (mər kyōōr´ ē əl) *adj.* quickly changing; volatile
Frank acted like an entirely different person sometimes because of his *mercurial* personality.
syn: fickle; unstable   *ant: unchanging; stable*

10. **exculpate** (ek´ skəl pāt) *v.* to clear of guilt; to declare innocent
The judge dismissed the case when new evidence *exculpated* the defendant.
syn: exonerate; acquit; vindicate   *ant: condemn; accuse; indict*

11. **salubrious** (sə lōō´ brē əs) *adj.* healthful
Each day, after lunch, Tammy took a *salubrious* walk through the park.
syn: salutary; wholesome   *ant: harmful; useless*

12. **vicissitude** (vi sis´ i tōōd) *n.* a sudden change or shift in one's life or circumstances
She claimed that her many *vicissitudes* throughout life had made her a stronger person.
syn: alteration; variation

13. **squelch** (skwelch) *v.* to suppress; squash
The candidate desperately tried to *squelch* rumors that he had once been arrested.
syn: extinguish; muffle; thwart   *ant: promote; support; enact*

14. **tyro** (tī´ rō) *n.* a beginner; novice
Until he learned the trade, the *tyro* was advised to keep his ears open and his thoughts to himself.
syn: amateur; neophyte; rookie   *ant: expert; master; guru*

15. **matriculate** (mə trik´ yə lāt) *v.* to admit or be admitted into a group or a college
Sam's grades were high enough for him to *matriculate* at State in the fall.

EXERCISE I—Words in Context

From the list below, supply the words needed to complete the paragraph. Some words will not be used.

tyro	arcane	nascent	sine qua non
vicissitudes	matriculate	bourgeois	

1. Steve cannot complain about where the _____ of life led him. His excellent academic record allowed him to _____ into the university of his choice, and he now enjoys a[n] _____ lifestyle, despite having grown up in abject poverty. Now, Steve earns his living as an anthropologist studying the _____ data of lost civilizations, though recent finds have given him a[n] _____ interest in treasure hunting.

From the list below, supply the words needed to complete the paragraph. Some words will not be used.

vicissitudes	tangential	tyro	squelch
exculpate	trenchant	paladin	

2. Debbie had the _____ qualities of a good leader, but she was still a[n] _____ at charity work and never expected to become the _____ of her cause. It was true that she had always had _____ interests in eliminating poverty in underdeveloped nations, but until she realized how rewarding the work was, she had _____ any interests in making a career out of it.

From the list below, supply the words needed to complete the paragraph. Some words will not be used.

indefeasible	arcane	sine qua non	mercurial
exculpate	salubrious	bourgeois	

3. "An extra pair of socks is a[n] _____ in making it to the end of this hike," said Mr. Bronson, the wilderness guide. "Your feet will be your greatest asset when we're twenty miles from civilization, and you'll need to exercise _____ habits to keep them in good shape for the duration of the week. No excuse will _____ you if you run out of socks or if your boots are too tight." The group about to embark on a week-long, 120-mile hike understood the guide's concern; there were enough natural hazards to worry about, such as _____ weather and poisonous snakes, without complicating matters more by making _____ mistakes on the trail.

EXERCISE II—Sentence Completion

Complete the sentence in a way that shows you understand the meaning of the italicized vocabulary word.

1. A healthy breakfast is a *sine qua non* for...

2. The prestigious university refused to *matriculate* the student until...

3. The doctor told Phil to find a *salubrious* hobby that...

4. The old storyteller had such a *trenchant* way of speaking that...

5. To limit media interference during the investigation, the police *squelched*...

6. On some days, the *mercurial* teacher was pleasant and soft spoken, but...

7. According to the Declaration of Independence, life, liberty, and the pursuit of happiness are *indefeasible* rights that cannot...

8. Denny is a *tyro* at riding a bicycle, so he...

9. Despite experiencing the *vicissitudes* of life during the war, every member of the family...

10. The eccentric professor took pride in his *arcane* knowledge of...

11. After the court *exculpated* Jack of any wrongdoing, he...

12. The princess, detained high within the castle, hoped that someday a *paladin* would...

13. The reporter wanted a straight answer, but the public relations clerk gave only *tangential* statements that...

14. Our increasingly technological society must protect itself against *nascent* threats of...

15. Some people prefer a *bourgeois* life to a wealthy life because they do not...

EXERCISE III—Roots, Prefixes, and Suffixes

Study the entries and answer the questions that follow.

The roots *path* means "feel" or "suffer."
The root *pass* means "endure" or "suffer."
The prefix *in* means "not."
The prefix *syn* means "together with."
The prefix *com* means "together with."
The prefix *tele* means "across."
The prefix *a* means "not" or "none."
The suffix *ic* means "pertaining to."

1. *Using literal translations as guidance, define the following words without using a dictionary.*

   A. compassion   D. telepathy
   B. impassive   E. apathy
   C. sympathy   F. passive

2. The prefix *en* means "in" or "into." What does the word *empathy* literally mean?

3. The word *pathetic* literally means _____.

4. *Passion* is another word for a strong _____.

5. List as many words as you can think of that contain the root *path*.

EXERCISE IV—Inference

Complete the sentences by inferring information about the italicized word from its context.

1. Tom's personality changed with each *vicissitude* he endured, because he...

2. If you are still a *tyro* at swimming long distances, you might think twice about...

3. A *nascent* way of doing something will probably not become popular until...

EXERCISE V—Critical Reading

Below is a pair of reading passages followed by several multiple-choice questions similar to the ones you will encounter on the SAT. Carefully read both passages and choose the best answer to each of the questions.

The authors of the following passages comment on the way in which technology influences the study of literature.

Passage 1

"Kids don't read enough" might sound like the anthem of any given English teacher, but suspend your bias for a few minutes and consider the facts. You might soon agree that television, movies, and other electronic media are, indeed, imperiling the critical thinking skills that only the study of literature affords.

5   The average American child spends between 22 and 28 hours a week watching television; that's four hours a day, every day, and that exempts factors that might increase viewing, such as unfavorable weather. Four hours of television—this is the daily diet of the average American TV watcher. It's enough to be a part-time job! When you throw in all the other electronic media, such as movies, music, radio,

10   etc., the number climbs to a brain-rotting six hours a day; six hours and nothing to show for it.

As people vegetate for increasingly long periods each day, the popularity of reading, of course, lags. Children under eighteen spend, on average, less than one hour a day reading, and behold, reading assessment scores are plummeting!

15   Coincidence?

The insidiousness of television can be attributed to its many attractions—perpetual action, simple story lines, and neat endings that reinforce expectations of quick and complete gratification. It is not surprising that the young hedonists in the making find it difficult to progress through a substantial work of literature, whether it's

20   a classic novel assigned in high school or a chapter book written for young students. It is becoming dangerously routine for writers to cater to diminished attention spans by "dumbing down" literature, thus giving it the effect of television commercials or erratic web pages. Internet summaries of novels are replacing the actual stories; after all, the authors obviously didn't mean to include all that extra non-

25   sense when they wrote the books.

Watching television, unlike reading, requires only a passive role from the viewer; reading, however, is both a physical and a mental skill. The physical process—literally taking in the information—can be modeled at home and taught at both home and at school. The mental process, by which readers internalize and interpret liter-

30   ature, must be developed one reader at a time. Developing the tangential skills to understand texts—increased vocabulary, orthography, interpretation—takes practice, and that means more reading. These fundamental skills eventually coalesce into critical-thinking skills, and grant readers the ability to anticipate, infer, and understand arguments and ideas in both texts and in any other form of communi-

35   cation.

Without the skills to interpret their own written language, people walk through a hazy world in which there are even fewer certainties than there are for people who do understand parts of it; they are like earthworms trying to understand the cackling of birds—hungry birds, perhaps. The paragons of literature—those books, sto-
40 ries, and novels that have inspired great people to do great things—are simply unavailable to those who cannot read them. So please, turn off the television, even if it's for only one of the four nightly hours, and read something. Your brains will thank you one day.

Passage 2

Don't waste your time reading books. In the present age, television, videos, and movies deliver literature twenty-four hours a day, and with all the immediacy of a newscast and the colors of a pageant.

The stories that have withstood the tests of time—the classics—did so because
5 they tell age-old human stories. "Man-versus-nature," "Man-versus-self," and "Man-versus-man" have been told and retold in so many thousands of ways that it's ridiculous even to create any new literature, let alone disallow the incorporation of these age-old themes into motion pictures that tell the same stories in much better ways than books. The film versions of *Ben-Hur, Antony and Cleopatra,* and *Lord of the*
10 *Flies* excited people just as the novels did when they were first released, and they eliminated the ponderous, literature-imposed obligation of having to sort out and understand characters without visual representation. Costumes, music, and visual clues in movies help viewers to differentiate characters, and stories, if convoluted, are easier to follow.
15 A transcendent acting performance can make a film version of a literary work much more memorable than the original printed version, and movies are often superior to texts because the language of the original is modernized. This opens a door through which the world can experience the great classics, which previously were only understandable to those people fluent in specialized languages and
20 dialects.

Publishers and booksellers will rarely, if ever, complain about movies reviving the popularity of certain books; they cash in on movie-based versions of books. Sometimes, these movie-books help original works to achieve a popularity that they never experienced on their own. Successful movies might line pockets in
25 Hollywood, but they certainly also boost the publishing industry.

With more than 98 percent of American homes owning at least one television set, the TV has replaced the book as a source of literature, and rightly so: by offering hundreds of channels, networks and cable companies are offering Americans a rich array of novels, drama, and nonfiction that's available all day, every day. Made-for-
30 TV movies, archived classics, and documentaries about movies ensure that a plethora of cultural knowledge is available to viewers everywhere.

Some critics worry that the transfer of literature from books to movies or equivalent electronic media will diminish thinking skills, but the concern is unnecessary because in most movie adaptations, clever scripts and subtle acting skills help

35 viewers to understand the plot. Television can only enhance vocabulary skills because most scripts maximize the use of mainstream words that represent the widest possible cross-section of American English dialect, which is what people need to know in order to function in society.

The literature that we know originated in oral tradition, by which stories were
40 relayed from one generation to the next. To make the stories memorable, story-tellers, bards, and poets sang, acted-out, or narrated dramatically, all of which ensured the perpetuation of their important messages. The modern film has taken the place of those itinerant storytellers in the mead halls of Europe, and it guarantees that the great legends will continue to entertain and educate indefinitely.

1. The tone of passage 1 is best described as
   A. doubtful.
   B. animated.
   C. detached.
   D. hostile.
   E. troubled.

2. As used in line 6 of passage 1, *exempts* most nearly means
   A. includes.
   B. divides.
   C. accounts.
   D. excludes.
   E. determines.

3. The *hedonists* mentioned in passage 1, paragraph 4, are people who
   A. learn quickly.
   B. seek pleasure.
   C. read profusely.
   D. debate television.
   E. employ teachers.

4. The simile in line 38 of passage 1 suggests that
   A. a lack of language skills can be dangerous.
   B. insects are higher-order animals than birds.
   C. mastering language skills is harder for some people than others.
   D. bird calls are a form of language.
   E. language skills are for those who want them.

5. In passage 2, paragraph 2, "Man-versus-nature," "Man-versus-self," and "Man-versus-man" are
   A. television shows about literature.
   B. categories for movie critics.
   C. ways for the author to express his misogyny.
   D. common thematic conflicts in literature.
   E. literary character types.

6. In line 15 of passage 2, *transcendent* means
   A. ridiculous.
   B. inspiring.
   C. transparent.
   D. ubiquitous.
   E. timeless.

7. Which choice best describes the author's intent in the following quotation from passage 2?

   > "Television can only enhance vocabulary skills because most scripts maximize the use of mainstream words that represent the widest possible cross-section of American English dialect, which is what people need to know in order to function in society."

   A. It portrays television's lack of challenging vocabulary words as a positive characteristic.
   B. It favorably describes the relationship between cable programming and current trends in education.
   C. It negatively portrays educators who rely upon literature-based films for classroom teaching.
   D. It supports the author's argument that literary works often share similar themes.
   E. It suggests that the author is a movie producer.

8. The purpose of the last paragraph of passage 2 is
   A. to inform about the history of drama.
   B. to suggest that television will soon replace books entirely.
   C. to create an emotional connection between readers and the cause of television.
   D. to determine whether readers benefit most from books or from television.
   E. to suggest that film is responsible for the continuation of literature.

9. The authors of both passages would agree that
    A. reading is extremely popular.
    B. movies are more entertaining than books.
    C. books are more entertaining than movies.
    D. television is extremely popular.
    E. educators should use television more often.

10. Which topic is in direct conflict between the two passages?
    A. the importance of vocabulary skills
    B. the prevalence of television viewers
    C. the effect of television on critical thinking skills
    D. challenges for educators teaching literature
    E. the history of literature

Lesson Seventeen

1. **depravity** (di prav´ i tē) *n.* moral corruption; perversion
    Megan was shocked by the *depravity* occurring on the reputable college's campus.
    syn: immorality; debauchery; vice   *ant: virtue; goodness; decency*

2. **megalomania** (meg ə lō mā´ nē ə) *n.* having delusions of grandeur; an obsession with grandiose things
    Bill's actual-sized, wood reproduction of the Great Pyramid is said to be the result of the unemployed carpenter's *megalomania*.

3. **attribute** (ə trib´ yōōt) *v.* to relate to a particular cause; to ascribe
    Tim, partially deaf at twenty-one, *attributes* his hearing loss to his loud car stereo.
    syn: credit; blame; impute   *ant: dismiss; absolve*

4. **celerity** (sə ler´ i tē) *n.* swiftness of action; speed
    The factory lost money every second it was shut down, so the engineers worked with great *celerity* to repair the huge machine on the assembly line.
    syn: haste; rapidity; alacrity   *ant: delay; procrastination*

5. **alimentary** (a lə men´ tə rē) *adj.* pertaining to food, nutrition, or digestion
    The doctor questioned Missy about her *alimentary* habits when she complained of frequent indigestion.
    syn: dietary; nutritive

6. **congenital** (kən jen´ i təl) *adj.* dating from birth; inherent or natural
    The child's *congenital* heart condition was minor, but it had to be monitored for the rest of her life.
    syn: inborn; inherent   *ant: acquired; contracted*

7. **discourse** (dis´ kôrs) *n.* a discussion; a conversation
    The suspect refused to engage in any *discourse* about the crime until his lawyer arrived.
    syn: communication

8. **primordial** (prī môr´ dē əl) *adj.* first in time; original
Long before the appearance of life, *primordial* Earth had a poisonous atmosphere and widespread volcanic activity.
syn: primeval; prehistoric   *ant: recent; current*

9. **remuneration** (ri myōō nə rā´ shən) *n.* compensation; payment
Clark demanded *remuneration* for having been brought to trial on false charges.
syn: recompense; restitution; reimbursement

10. **attenuate** (ə ten´ ū āt) *v.* to reduce, weaken, or lessen
The drought *attenuated* the mighty river until it was a mere stream.
syn: diminish; shrink; reduce   *ant: strengthen; increase; intensify*

11. **mutable** (myōō´ tə bəl) *adj.* subject to change
Pack an assortment of clothes, because the weather in the mountains is *mutable*.
syn: variable; inconstant; unstable   *ant: consistent; constant; steady;*
                                                   immutable

12. **ethereal** (i thēr´ ē əl) *adj.* light or airy; intangible; heavenly
The subjects of Michelangelo's paintings often have an *ethereal* beauty.
syn: celestial; impalpable; unearthly   *ant: heavy; thick; substantial*

13. **encomium** (en kō´ mē əm) *n.* formal praise; a tribute
The publisher hoped that the author's first novel would receive an *encomium* from the demanding critic.
syn: acclaim; endorsement; commendation   *ant: insult; condemnation*

14. **tactile** (tak´ təl) *adj.* pertaining to the sense of touch
Roger still had *tactile* senses in his paralyzed legs, indicating that he had a good chance of walking again.

15. **ascetic** (ə set´ ik) *n.* a person who renounces material comforts and practices extreme self-denial
The ancient fortune-teller was an *ascetic* who often abstained from food for days without complaint.

EXERCISE I—Words in Context

From the list below, supply the words needed to complete the paragraph. Some words will not be used.

attenuate	depravity	remuneration	primordial
encomiums	discourse	ethereal	

1. Paige, a researcher who had earned the _____ of the pharmaceutical industry for her accomplishments, frequently traveled to the jungles of Peru in pursuit of a natural compound thought to _____ the torturous side effects of chemotherapy. The jungle fascinated Paige; its thick vegetation and enormous plants gave her a sense of what the _____ forests of Earth must have looked like when dinosaurs grazed on treetops and the ground rumbled with volcanic activity. In the evenings, Paige usually sat quietly at her camp and watched as the fog crept slowly down the verdant hills and settled in the valley, blanketing the old forest in a[n] _____ haze, like something out of a dream. To Paige, witnessing such natural beauty was ample _____ for her hard work.

From the list below, supply the words needed to complete the paragraph. Some words will not be used.

ethereal	ascetic	congenital	depravity
attribute	megalomania	mutable	

2. During the new mayor's campaign, he claimed to be a political _____ with the goal of reducing all wasteful government spending and _____ within the ranks of the city government; however, the mayor's promises must have been _____ because his first action as mayor was to approve the construction of an unnecessary new park. Critics _____ the expensive project to the new mayor's _____, which was explained further when the mayor published his self-promoting autobiography.

From the list below, supply the words needed to complete the paragraph. Some words will not be used.

remuneration	celerity	alimentary	congenital
attribute	discourse	tactile	

3.   All of Mike's _____ senses were still numbed after the surgery, but he was able to hear the _____ between his wife and the surgeon. The _____ stomach condition that had interfered with Mike's _____ processes since he was a baby had been corrected, and Mike would simply need plenty of rest to heal with _____.

EXERCISE II—Sentence Completion

Complete the sentence in a way that shows you understand the meaning of the italicized vocabulary word.

1.   Kristen was awed by the *ethereal* sight of...

2.   *Depravity* in the organization eventually caused...

3.   *Discourse* among the students suddenly stopped when...

4.   Dave, who frequently indulged in gourmet pleasures, called his wife an *ascetic* because she refused to...

5.   The plans are *mutable*, so be prepared to...

6.   Tim's *megalomania* makes life difficult for his friends because he is constantly...

7.   The archaeologist found fossils of *primordial* microorganisms when she...

8.   The safecracker wore gloves whenever he wasn't working so that his *tactile* senses would be sharp enough to...

9.   *Celerity* of work was important to the construction crew because...

10. Lisa enjoyed the *encomium* from all the townspeople for...

11. After the recall, the automobile manufacturer said that *remunerations* would be provided for anyone who...

12. Logan *attributes* crop circles to UFOs, but most of his friends…

13. An earthworm's *alimentary* process is…

14. The high rate of *congenital* birth defects in the area was blamed on…

15. The rising costs of building supplies *attenuated* the couple's desire to…

EXERCISE III—Roots, Prefixes, and Suffixes

Study the entries and answer the questions that follow.

The roots *grad* and *gress* mean "step."
The roots *ced* and *cess* mean "go."
The prefix *de* means "down."
The prefix *pro* means "forward."
The prefix *re* means "back."
The prefix *di* means "apart" or "away from."
The prefix *trans* means "across" or "through."

1. *Using literal translations as guidance, define the following words without using a dictionary.*

   A. regression
   B. procession
   C. digress
   D. recede
   E. degrade
   F. progression

2. The prefix *se* means "away." In the 1860s, the Confederate States tried to _____ (literally, "go away") from the Union.

3. A synonym for *sin* that literally means "stepping across the line" is

   _____.

4. If the prefix *ex* means "outside," what does the word *exceed* literally mean?

5. List as many words as you can think of that contain the roots *ced* or *cess.*

6. List as many words as you can think of that contain the roots *grad* or *gress.*

EXERCISE IV—Inference

Complete the sentences by inferring information about the italicized word from its context.

1. The fire chief *attributed* the blaze to faulty wiring, so the police had no need to...

2. An *ascetic* who eats roots, sleeps on the floor, and drinks only water, would probably decline an invitation to...

3. If father refuses to partake in any further *discourse* on the subject, then he does not want to...

EXERCISE V—Writing

Here is a writing prompt similar to the one you will find on the writing portion of the SAT.

Plan and write an essay based on the following statement:

Virtue is like a rich stone, best plain set.
–Francis Bacon (1561–1626)

Assignment: Francis Bacon suggests that virtue, like a fine diamond, requires no decorative enhancement. In an essay, explain the purpose of Francis Bacon's statement, identify whether you agree or disagree with it, and include an example of the behavior that Bacon alludes to. Support your essay using an example from literature, history, current events, or your experience or observation.

Thesis: Write a one-sentence response to the above assignment. Make certain this sentence offers a clear statement of your position.

Example: Advertising one's virtue, or demonstrating it unnecessarily, can compromise its value.

Organizational Plan: If your thesis is the point on which you want to end, where does your essay need to begin? List the points of development that are inevitable in leading your reader from your beginning point to your end point. This list is your outline.

Draft: Use your thesis as both your beginning and your end. Following your outline, write a good first draft of your essay. Remember to support all of your points with examples, facts, references to reading, etc.

Review and revise: Exchange essays with a classmate. Using the scoring guide for Word Choice on page 251, score your partner's essay (while he or she scores yours). Focus on word choice and the use of language conventions. If necessary, rewrite your essay to improve your word choice and your use of language.

Identifying Sentence Errors

Identify the grammatical error in each of the following sentences. If the sentence contains no error, select answer E.

1. We <u>saved enough money</u> from the previous <u>three month's paychecks</u>, and
      (A)   (B)
    we can <u>finally afford</u> to <u>go on a long vacation to</u> Rome.   <u>No error</u>
             (C)   (D)   (E)

2. Last <u>April, members</u> of the <u>senior class took</u> a trip from <u>Buffalo to</u>
          (A)   (B)   (C)
    <u>Niagara Falls, New York,</u> and then across the border to <u>Toronto Canada.</u>
                                                                    (D)

    <u>No error</u>
    (E)

3. We <u>visited Tom</u> in the hospital after his <u>car accident;</u> he <u>seemed good,</u>
         (A)   (B)   (C)
    and the broken bones <u>are almost completely healed.</u>   <u>No error</u>
                          (D)   (E)

4. <u>Although</u> the elderly King James died last week after a long <u>illness, his</u>
    (A)   (B)
    son <u>will legally</u> become <u>the new ruler of the country.</u>   <u>No error</u>
         (C)   (D)   (E)

5. Larry <u>could have</u> <u>freezed</u> to death in last <u>winter's terrible blizzard, but</u>
           (A)   (B)   (C)
    he <u>survived.</u>   <u>No error</u>
       (D)   (E)

Improving Sentences

The underlined portion of each sentence below contains some flaw. Select the
answer that best corrects the flaw.

6. Neither Charlotte nor her sisters is going to the mall.
    A. Neither Charlotte or her sisters is going to the mall.
    B. Neither Charlotte nor her sisters are going to the mall.
    C. Charlotte and her sisters are not going to the mall.
    D. Neither Charlotte and her sister are going to the mall.
    E. Neither of Charlotte's sisters are going to the mall.

7. The assistance of two electricians, one network administrator, an infor-
    mation technology specialist, and three helpers were necessary to fix all
    the computer errors that had caused the crash.
    A. was necessary to fix all the computer errors that had caused the
        crash.
    B. were necessary to fix the computer errors that caused the crash.
    C. were necessary to fix all the computer errors, which had caused the
        crash.
    D. was necessary to fix each and every one of the errors that had caused
        the computer to crash.
    E. fixed all the computer errors that crashed.

8. One thing I know that will keep me from traveling abroad, and those are
    the high costs of flying.
    A. I know one thing that will keep me from traveling abroad—the high
        cost of flying.
    B. One thing that I know that will keep me from traveling overseas, are
        the high costs of flying.
    C. I know one thing keeping me from traveling abroad, and that is the
        risks of flying.
    D. Flying and the high costs of doing so are some of the major things I
        know that will keep me from traveling abroad.
    E. Traveling abroad and the high costs of flying will keep me from
        doing these things, I know that.

9. He is as strong, if not stronger than his father.
    A. He is as strong, if not stronger then his father was.
    B. He is strong, as is his father.
    C. He is as strong, if not more strong than his father.
    D. He is as strong as, if not stronger then his father.
    E. He is as strong as his father, if not stronger.

10. An aspiring pianist should spend hours <u>practicing; otherwise you will</u>
    <u>never be successful.</u>
    A. practicing otherwise you will never be successful.
    B. practicing because otherwise, you will never be successful.
    C. practicing; otherwise he or she will never be successful.
    D. in practicing; otherwise you will never be a success.
    E. practicing, or else you will never be successful.

Lesson Eighteen

1. **poignant** (poin´ yənt) *adj.* very moving; touching
The movie would be simply mediocre if it didn't contain an especially *poignant* scene.
syn: emotional; affecting; sentimental   *ant: unemotional; cold*

2. **venial** (vē´ nē əl) *adj.* easily excused or forgiven
A *venial* offense such as jaywalking usually bears little or no fine.
syn: pardonable; remittable; excusable   *ant: inexcusable; unforgivable*

3. **satiate** (sā´ shē āt) *v.* to satisfy fully
No amount of riches could *satiate* the greedy baron.
syn: gratify; suit

4. **vituperative** (vī tōō´ pə rə tiv) *adj.* fault-finding; verbally abusive
The *vituperative* drill instructor screamed at the new recruit for not having shiny boots and a pressed uniform.
syn: castigating; derisive; scathing   *ant: flattering; sweet; kind*

5. **cumulative** (kyōō´ myə lə tiv) *adj.* resulting from accumulation; increasing
Her *cumulative* grade point average, from the ninth grade to the present, is 3.7.
syn: aggregate; summative; collective   *ant: decreasing; subtracting*

6. **exhilaration** (ig zil´ ə rā´ shən) *n.* thrill; invigoration
A sense of *exhilaration* overwhelmed me as I reached the summit and looked down at the forest far below.
syn: excitement; elation   *ant: boredom; apathy; ennui*

7. **pundit** (pun´ dit) *n.* a critic
The political *pundit* commented on government actions each morning on a radio show.
syn: commentator; reviewer; analyzer

8. **propriety** (prə prī´ i tē) *n.* proper behavior; appropriateness
The man carried himself with such *propriety* that few would have guessed he was homeless.
syn: decency; etiquette; seemliness   *ant: rudeness; indecency*

9. **goad** (gōd) *v.* to urge forward; to prod
The kids in the schoolyard *goaded* the boy into sticking his tongue to the frozen flagpole.
syn: spur; press; incite　　　　　　*ant: deter; discourage; dissuade*

10. **impunity** (im pyōō´ ni tē) *n.* freedom from punishment, penalty, or harm
No one can speak against the king with *impunity*.
syn: immunity; liberty　　　　　　*ant: vulnerability; risk*

11. **surfeit** (sûr´ fit) *n.* an excessive amount
A *surfeit* of oranges this year drove the price down.
syn: excess; overabundance; surplus　　　　*ant: shortage; dearth; deficiency*

12. **trite** (trīt) *adj.* overused; hackneyed; clichéd
I could tell by my agent's *trite* reply that she hadn't actually read my manuscript.
syn: banal; routine; timeworn　　　　　*ant: fresh; provocative; original*

13. **extricate** (ek´ stri kāt) *v.* to release; to disentangle
The escape artist *extricated* himself from the chains holding him under water in less than one minute.
syn: free; deliver; liberate　　　　　*ant: entangle; hinder*

14. **superfluous** (sōō pûr´ flōō əs) *adj.* unnecessary; excessive
The new luxury SUV had many *superfluous* options, including two televisions.
syn: exorbitant; gratuitous; extravagant　　*ant: essential; necessary; imperative*

15. **lithe** (līth) *adj.* graceful in motion; moving and bending with ease
The *lithe* gymnast's movements were graceful and seemingly effortless.
syn: agile; flowing; supple　　　　　*ant: rigid; clumsy; awkward*

EXERCISE I—Words in Context

From the list below, supply the words needed to complete the paragraph. Some words will not be used.

surfeit	lithe	superfluous	satiate
pundit	trite	vituperative	

1. The author knew that his novel was far from great, but according to the _____ reviews of numerous _____, the book was simply awful. Most critics noted that the detective thriller contains a[n] _____ of _____ expressions that could have been stolen from the script of any low-budget action film, and that the author used little creativity in allowing the hero of the novel, Lance Driver, to solve most of his problems through the use of _____ violence.

From the list below, supply the words needed to complete the paragraph. Some words will not be used.

extricate	pundit	venial	exhilaration
poignant	goad	lithe	

2. Two months after the tragic bridge collapse, the lone survivor told her _____ survival tale to a newspaper reporter. Sharon had been wounded when the roadway surface of the bridge fell more than sixty feet to the water, but luckily she was _____ enough to _____ herself from the mangled wreckage of the bridge and her car. Feeling the pain of multiple fractures, Sharon crawled up a fallen steel girder with only the thought of seeing her family again to _____ her. She recalls the _____ she felt when she first saw the rescue helicopter approaching; however, the feeling was short-lived because Sharon quickly passed out from shock.

From the list below, supply the words needed to complete the paragraph. Some words will not be used.

vituperative	cumulative	impunity	satiate
propriety	exhilaration	venial	

3.   To Randy's parents, wasting hard-earned money was no _____ crime. When Randy was six years old, his parents opened a savings account for him. Over the years, the _____ balance rose to the thousands of dollars, but Randy could not touch it unless he proved that he would demonstrate _____ in handling the money. On occasion, Randy was allowed to use some of it to _____ his need to increase the size of his baseball card collection, but he was certainly never allowed to go to the mall and spend with _____; the money was meant to pay for college, after all.

EXERCISE II—Sentence Completion

Complete the sentence in a way that shows you understand the meaning of the italicized vocabulary word.

1.   Each morning, the *pundit* scanned the newspaper to find...

2.   Every time Roslyn watches that *poignant* black-and-white movie, she...

3.   Frank harvested a *surfeit* of tomatoes from his garden this year, so he...

4.   Cal stopped allowing his dog to run free in the woods after he had to *extricate* the animal from...

5.   The mobsters operated the illegal casino with *impunity* until...

6.   When a bowling ball fell on Dad's foot after he opened the closet, he broke into a series of *vituperative* screams about...

7.   Shannon had to avoid any *superfluous* expenses until she...

8   The new supervisor didn't mind if workers committed *venial* errors, but if when they began to make mistakes that cost the company money, she...

9.   The cover of the greeting card featured a *trite* expression about...

10. Before the field trip, the teacher warned the students that anyone who fails to represent the school with *propriety* would...

11. Ben didn't eat enough to *satiate* himself because he didn't want to...

12. Brad lived for experiencing the *exhilaration* of...

13. After twenty years of working with uranium, Steve's *cumulative* radiation exposure finally...

14. The crowd stared at the almost hypnotic movements of the *lithe*...

15. Craig had never been swimming, so his parents had to *goad* him to...

EXERCISE III—Roots, Prefixes, and Suffixes

Study the entries and answer the questions that follow.

The roots *ag* and *act* mean "to do" or "drive."
The roots *mov* and *mot* mean "to move."
The prefix *de* means "down."
The prefix *in* means "not."
The prefix *pro* means "forward."

1. *Using literal translations as guidance, define the following words without using a dictionary.*

   A. promote   D. proactive
   B. inactive   E. immovable
   C. demote   F. agitate

2. The prefix *com* means "together." What does the word *commotion* literally mean?

3. If a story *moves* you, then it might cause you to experience a particular _____, or feeling.

4. *Mob* is another form of the root *mov*. List as many words as you can think of that contain the root *mob*.

5. List as many words as you can think of that contain the roots *mov* or *mot*.

EXERCISE IV—Inference

Complete the sentences by inferring information about the italicized word from its context.

1. A teacher might overlook a student's *venial* faults if the student...

2. If the fishermen have to *extricate* a dolphin from the fishing net, then the dolphin must be...

3. Ambassadors must demonstrate great *propriety* while meeting with foreign officials because...

EXERCISE V—Critical Reading

Below is a reading passage followed by several multiple-choice questions similar to the ones you will encounter on the SAT. Carefully read the passage and choose the best answer to each of the questions.

The following passage is an excerpt from Jane Eyre, *an extremely popular novel by Victorian author Charlotte Brontë (1816–1855).* Jane Eyre, *written in 1847, is fiction, but it contains significant autobiographical elements.*

Ere the half-hour ended, five o'clock struck; school was dismissed, and all were gone into the refectory to tea. I now ventured to descend: it was deep dusk; I retired into a corner and sat down on the floor. The spell by which I had been so far supported began to dissolve; reaction took place, and soon, so overwhelming was the
5   grief that seized me, I sank prostrate with my face to the ground. Now I wept: Helen Burns was not here; nothing sustained me; left to myself I abandoned myself, and my tears watered the boards. I had meant to be so good, and to do so much at Lowood: to make so many friends, to earn respect and win affection. Already I had made visible progress: that very morning I had reached the head of my class; Miss
10 Miller had praised me warmly; Miss Temple had smiled approbation; she had promised to teach me drawing, and to let me learn French, if I continued to make similar improvement two months longer: and then I was well received by my fellow-pupils; treated as an equal by those of my own age, and not molested by any; now, here I lay again crushed and trodden on; and could I ever rise more?
15 "Never," I thought; and ardently I wished to die. While sobbing out this wish in broken accents, some one approached: I started up—again Helen Burns was near me; the fading fires just showed her coming up the long, vacant room; she brought my coffee and bread.

"Come, eat something," she said; but I put both away from me, feeling as if a
20 drop or a crumb would have choked me in my present condition. Helen regarded me, probably with surprise: I could not now abate my agitation, though I tried hard; I continued to weep aloud. She sat down on the ground near me, embraced her knees with her arms, and rested her head upon them; in that attitude she remained silent as an Indian. I was the first who spoke.

25 "Helen, why do you stay with a girl whom everybody believes to be a liar?"

"Everybody, Jane? Why, there are only eighty people who have heard you called so, and the world contains hundreds of millions."

"But what have I to do with millions? The eighty, I know, despise me."

"Jane, you are mistaken: probably not one in the school either despises or dis-
30 likes you: many, I am sure, pity you much."

"How can they pity me after what Mr. Brocklehurst has said?"

"Mr. Brocklehurst is not a god: nor is he even a great and admired man: he is little liked here; he never took steps to make himself liked. Had he treated you as an especial favorite, you would have found enemies, declared or covert, all around
35 you; as it is, the greater number would offer you sympathy if they dared. Teachers and pupils may look coldly on you for a day or two, but friendly feelings are

concealed in their hearts; and if you persevere in doing well, these feelings will ere long appear so much the more evidently for their temporary suppression. Besides, Jane"—she paused.

40   "Well, Helen?" said I, putting my hand into hers: she chafed my fingers gently to warm them, and went on.

"If all the world hated you, and believed you wicked, while your own conscience approved you, and absolved you from guilt, you would not be without friends."

"No; I know I should think well of myself; but that is not enough: if others don't

45   love me I would rather die than live—I cannot bear to be solitary and hated, Helen. Look here; to gain some real affection from you, or Miss Temple, or any other whom I truly love, I would willingly submit to have the bone of my arm broken, or to let a bull toss me, or to stand behind a kicking horse, and let it dash its hoof at my chest—"

50   "Hush, Jane! You think too much of the love of human beings; you are too impulsive, too vehement; the sovereign hand that created your frame, and put life into it, has provided you with other resources than your feeble self, or than creatures feeble as you. Besides this earth, and besides the race of men, there is an invisible world and a kingdom of spirits: that world is round us, for it is everywhere;

55   and those spirits watch us, for they are commissioned to guard us; and if we were dying in pain and shame, if scorn smote us on all sides, and hatred crushed us, angels see our tortures, recognize our innocence (if innocent we be: as I know you are of this charge which Mr. Brocklehurst has weakly and pompously repeated at second-hand from Mrs. Reed; for I read a sincere nature in your ardent eyes and on

60   your clear front), and God waits only the separation of spirit from flesh to crown us with a full reward. Why, then, should we ever sink overwhelmed with distress, when life is so soon over, and death is so certain an entrance to happiness—to glory?"

I was silent; Helen had calmed me; but in the tranquility she imparted there was

65   an alloy of inexpressible sadness. I felt the impression of woe as she spoke, but I could not tell whence it came; and when, having done speaking, she breathed a little fast and coughed a short cough, I momentarily forgot my own sorrows to yield to a vague concern for her.

Resting my head on Helen's shoulder, I put my arms round her waist; she drew

70   me to her, and we reposed in silence. We had not sat long thus, when another person came in. Some heavy clouds, swept from the sky by a rising wind, had left the moon bare; and her light, streaming in through a window near, shone full both on us and on the approaching figure, which we at once recognized as Miss Temple.

"I came on purpose to find you, Jane Eyre," said she; "I want you in my room;

75   and as Helen Burns is with you, she may come too."

We went; following the superintendent's guidance, we had to thread some intricate passages, and mount a staircase before we reached her apartment; it contained a good fire, and looked cheerful. Miss Temple told Helen Burns to be seated in a low armchair on one side of the hearth, and herself taking another, she called me

80   to her side.

"Is it all over?" she asked, looking down at my face. "Have you cried your grief away?"

"I am afraid I never shall do that."

"Why?"

85   "Because I have been wrongly accused; and you, ma'am, and everybody else, will now think me wicked."

"We shall think you what you prove yourself to be, my child. Continue to act as a good girl, and you will satisfy us."

"Shall I, Miss Temple?"

90   "You will," said she, passing her arm round me. "And now tell me who is the lady whom Mr. Brocklehurst called your benefactress?"

"Mrs. Reed, my uncle's wife. My uncle is dead, and he left me to her care."

"Did she not, then, adopt you of her own accord?"

"No, ma'am; she was sorry to have to do it: but my uncle, as I have often heard
95 the servants say, got her to promise before he died that she would always keep me."

"Well now, Jane, you know, or at least I will tell you, that when a criminal is accused, he is always allowed to speak in his own defense. You have been charged with falsehood; defend yourself to me as well as you can. Say whatever your memory suggests is true; but add nothing and exaggerate nothing."

100   I resolved, in the depth of my heart, that I would be most moderate—most correct; and, having reflected a few minutes in order to arrange coherently what I had to say, I told her all the story of my sad childhood. Exhausted by emotion, my language was more subdued than it generally was when it developed that sad theme; and mindful of Helen's warnings against the indulgence of resentment, I infused
105 into the narrative far less of gall and wormwood than ordinary. Thus restrained and simplified, it sounded more credible: I felt as I went on that Miss Temple fully believed me.

In the course of the tale I had mentioned Mr. Lloyd as having come to see me after the fit: for I never forgot the, to me, frightful episode of the red-room: in
110 detailing which, my excitement was sure, in some degree, to break bounds; for nothing could soften in my recollection the spasm of agony which clutched my heart when Mrs. Reed spurned my wild supplication for pardon, and locked me a second time in the dark and haunted chamber.

I had finished: Miss Temple regarded me a few minutes in silence; she then said,
115 "I know something of Mr. Lloyd; I shall write to him; if his reply agrees with your statement, you shall be publicly cleared from every imputation; to me, Jane, you are clear now."

1. The narrator of this passage is
    A. Jane, a school-aged girl
    B. Mrs. Reed, Jane's aunt.
    C. Helen, a student.
    D. Mr. Brocklehurst, the schoolmaster.
    E. Miss Temple, the superintendent.

2. Helen Burns is probably
    A. Jane's guardian angel.
    B. Jane's sister.
    C. Jane's guidance counselor.
    D. Jane's friend.
    E. Jane's English teacher.

3. Helen warns Jane about befriending Mr. Brocklehurst because
    A. Mr. Brocklehurst is the superintendent.
    B. it would cause people to dislike Jane.
    C. Mr. Brocklehurst does not like Helen.
    D. he is an acquaintance of Jane's family.
    E. Mr. Brocklehurst is the schoolmaster.

4. According to the passage, Jane was
    A. caught in a lie.
    B. playing in the classroom and got into a fight.
    C. fighting with someone in the hall.
    D. accused of something that she did not do.
    E. accused of something that Helen did.

5. Which statement best demonstrates the intended idea of the following quotation?

    > "If all the world hated you, and believed you wicked, while
    > your own conscience approved you, and absolved you
    > from guilt, you would not be without friends."

    A. Friends will always believe you, as long as you believe yourself.
    B. No one needs friends.
    C. You always have a friend in yourself.
    D. You cannot count on friends to bail you out.
    E. Only what you think is important, unless you think yourself to be guilty.

6. As used in line 65, *alloy* most nearly means
   A. binary number.
   B. blending.
   C. metal.
   D. truce.
   E. contaminant.

7. Which choice best paraphrases the following quotation?

   > "…mindful of Helen's warnings against the indulgence of resentment, I infused into the narrative far less of gall and wormwood than ordinary."

   A. Being mindful of Helen's warning about spite, I focused on positive things during my explanation.
   B. I left out the bad things during my explanation because it is not good to be resented.
   C. The resentment that I had for Helen did not stop me from infusing the ordinary nerve into my story.
   D. Heeding Helen's warning about being resentful, I made my account less spiteful than it might have typically been.
   E. Helen's warning about resentment allowed me to be polite, as usual, during my narrative.

8. The story in this passage takes place
   A. in the morning, before school begins.
   B. at lunchtime, while Jane and Helen are waiting for their next class.
   C. in the early afternoon, before Mr. Brocklehurst returns from vacation.
   D. at night, after school has let out for the day.
   E. on Saturday, while Jane is in detention for lying on Friday.

9. This passage would likely be found in
   A. a newspaper column.
   B. a book report.
   C. a self-help book about friendship.
   D. a novel.
   E. a history textbook.

10. The most appropriate title for this passage would be
    A. A Day at School.
    B. Worry Not, Jane.
    C. Being the New Girl.
    D. Miss Temple's Mistake.
    E. White Lies.

Lesson Nineteen

1. **stentorian** (sten tôr´ ē ən) *adj.* extremely loud
   The lieutenant repeated the general's orders in a *stentorian* voice that could be heard by the entire regiment.
   syn: blaring; booming; roaring   *ant: quiet; muted*

2. **propitious** (prō pish´ əs) *adj.* promising; auspicious
   The gold doubloon was a *propitious* discovery for the explorers because it meant that the treasure was nearby.
   syn: favorable; advantageous; beneficial   *ant: ominous; harmful; unfortunate*

3. **transient** (tran´ zē ənt) *adj.* remaining only a short time
   The restaurant owner treated the regular customers better than she did the *transient* customers, who probably wouldn't return.
   syn: temporary; fleeting; provisional   *ant: permanent; enduring*

4. **tremulous** (trem´ yə ləs) *adj.* timid; fearful
   Afraid of being rejected, he asked her for a date in a *tremulous* voice.
   syn: anxious; sheepish; nervous   *ant: brave; confident; bold*

5. **fulsome** (fŏŏl´ səm) *adj.* offensively flattering; insincere
   The driver smirked and made a *fulsome* compliment to his opponent before the race.
   syn: unctuous; ingratiating; fawning   *ant: sincere; heartfelt*

6. **utilitarian** (yōō til ə târ´ ē ən) *adj.* useful; practical
   The hermit's *utilitarian* cabin provided shelter from the weather and a place to store food, but little else.
   syn: practical; functional   *ant: useless*

7. **schism** (siz´ əm) *n.* a separation or division
   The political party experienced a severe *schism* when members disagreed about how best to distribute the funds.
   syn: break; estrangement; split   *ant: unification; merger; alliance*

8. **rescind** (ri sind´) *v.* to repeal; to make void
   Congress was forced to *rescind* the unconstitutional law.
   syn: recall; repeal; nullify   *ant: adopt; enact; promote*

9. **extant** (ek´ stənt) *adj.* still in existence
    Despite the effectiveness of modern medicine, home remedies and the
    use of healing herbs are still *extant.*
    syn: existent; present; remaining   *ant: extinct; dead; gone*

10. **inchoate** (in kō´ it) *adj.* not yet complete; undeveloped
    He thought that with a little refining, his *inchoate* idea could easily
    become the invention of the century.
    syn: rudimentary; preliminary; unformed   *ant: refined; shaped; developed*

11. **unwieldy** (un wēl´ dē) *adj.* not easily carried because of size, shape,
    or complexity
    It took an hour to carry the *unwieldy* couch up the stairs to the
    apartment.
    syn: awkward; cumbersome; ungainly   *ant: convenient; manageable*

12. **spurious** (spyŭr´ ē əs) *adj.* possible but ultimately false; not genuine
    The evidence did not comply with the defendant's *spurious* testimony.
    syn: counterfeit; bogus   *ant: legitimate; genuine; authentic*

13. **abjure** (ab jŭr´) *v.* to renounce or recant
    During a public rally, the dictator forced the writer to *abjure* his criticism
    of the government.
    syn: retract; revoke   *ant: assert; maintain; endorse*

14. **inveterate** (in vet´ ər it) *adj.* habitual; continuing
    The *inveterate* criminal didn't retire until he was incarcerated.
    syn: chronic

15. **dissipate** (dis´ ə pāt) *v.* to waste recklessly; to exhaust
    It took only one month for the irresponsible son to *dissipate* his
    inheritance.
    syn: squander; misuse   *ant: save; conserve*

EXERCISE I—Words in Context

From the list below, supply the words needed to complete the paragraph. Some words will not be used.

dissipate	inchoate	propitious	rescind
extant	transient	unwieldy	

1. The tropical storm struck with swift fury; a rogue wave had destroyed the tiny ship's wheelhouse and pulled both the skipper and the first mate overboard into the raging sea. The engine and radio had been rendered inoperable, and the only _____ supplies consisted of a single case of bottled water and a small cooler containing sandwiches.

   "We don't know how long we'll be adrift, so we cannot _____ our limited food supply," said Nancy, as the passengers stared horrified at the broken glass lying on the deck where the wheelhouse once stood. Jack, who at least had a[n] _____ knowledge of mechanics, fiddled with the engine in an attempt to get it to run. That night, passengers helplessly watched the _____ lights of ships passing in the distance, but had no means of signaling them. Early the next morning, passengers awoke to the _____ sound of the ship's engine sputtering and then, miraculously, running.

From the list below, supply the words needed to complete the paragraph. Some words will not be used.

dissipate	spurious	unwieldy	schism
inveterate	abjure	stentorian	

2. Bill and Ted had been friends for twenty years, until falling in love with the same woman caused a[n] _____ that drove them apart. Though the woman had no interest in either of the men and had long ago departed the small town, a[n] _____ contempt remained between the former pals for years. When they inadvertently crossed paths with one another around town or at the grocery store, Bill and Ted exchanged _____ greetings that did little to hide their mutual scorn. It took twelve years for the two men to _____ their dislike for each other and cast off the _____ grudge that had burdened them throughout their lives.

From the list below, supply the words needed to complete the paragraph. Some words will not be used.

rescind	**extant**	**fulsome**	**stentorian**
utilitarian	**tremulous**	**schism**	

3.   Ryan was just about to doze off when a[n] _____ announcement blasted over the intercom, causing some of the more _____ passengers to sit up straight in their coach-class seats. In his most _____ voice, the captain thanked the passengers for flying the airline and then _____ his previous estimate that the flight would be late; passengers could expect to arrive in Anchorage in less than one hour. The news pleased Ryan; if the flight arrived early, he would have ample time to prepare for his important business meeting. He smiled as he slipped his notebook computer into a[n] _____ leather briefcase and buckled his seatbelt.

EXERCISE II—Sentence Completion

Complete the sentence in a way that shows you understand the meaning of the italicized vocabulary word.

1. Phil had only *transient* exposure to the contagious patients, so he didn't worry about…

2. Jill wants a *utilitarian* family car, but her husband wants…

3. The campers could not *dissipate* their supplies because they…

4. Vicky replaced her *unwieldy* purse with one that…

5. When a *schism* resulted over the best way to find the trail, half of the lost hikers…

6. The angry teacher made a *stentorian* request for the students to…

7. During the questioning, the captured soldier created a *spurious* story that…

8. The corporation hired a lobbyist to convince the government to *rescind* legislation that…

9. To the crew of the marooned ship, a bird carrying nesting materials was a *propitious* sign that…

10. When new discoveries proved him wrong, the scientist was driven to *abjure*…

11. Mike, an *inveterate* joker, constantly thinks about…

12. The *tremulous* man could not bring himself to…

13. The novel will remain *inchoate* until the author…

14. The boss hated hearing the *fulsome* comments of employees who were simply trying to…

15. The supports of the century-old railroad bridge are still *extant*, despite…

EXERCISE III—Roots, Prefixes, and Suffixes

Study the entries and answer the questions that follow.

The root *mis* means "hatred."
The root *bio* means "life."
The root *morph* means "shape."
The root *anthrop* means "human."
The suffix *logy* means "study of."
The prefix *meta* means "change."
The prefix *anti* means "against."
The prefix *a* means "not" or "none."

1. Using literal translations as guidance, define the following words without using a dictionary.

    A. anthropomorphic   D. antibiotic
    B. metamorphosis   E. biology
    C. anthropology   F. amorphous

2. The root *graph* means "writing." What does the word *biography* literally mean?

3. There is a special branch of linguistics (the study of language) called *morphology*. Explain the probable purpose of this branch.

4. A[n] _____ has a hatred for his or her fellow human beings.

5. List as many words as you can think of that contain the root *bio*.

EXERCISE IV—Inference

Complete the sentences by inferring information about the italicized word from its context.

1. Someone who has an *inchoate* understanding of electricity should not...

2. Your present jacket might look nice on you in the Arctic, but you'll need to replace it with a *utilitarian* coat that...

3. To get the *unwieldy* box from the store to your home, you might need to...

EXERCISE V—Writing

Here is a writing prompt similar to the one you will find on the writing portion of the SAT.

Plan and write an essay based on the following statement:

> Let us honor if we can
> The vertical man,
> Though we value none
> But the horizontal one.

> –W.H. Auden: *Shorts*

Assignment: Do you agree or disagree with Auden's suggestion about how and when people are appreciated by others? In an essay, use your own language to translate Auden's statement, and explain why you do or do not agree with it. Support your essay using examples from literature, history, current events, or your experience and observation.

Thesis: Write a one-sentence response to the above assignment. Make certain this single sentence offers a clear statement of your position.

Example: Auden appropriately suggests that great people are seldom appreciated while they are alive, but there are many exceptions to this practice.

Organizational Plan: If your thesis is the point on which you want to end, where does your essay need to begin? List the points of development that are inevitable in leading your reader from your beginning point to your end point. This list is your outline.

Draft: Use your thesis as both your beginning and your end. Following your outline, write a good first draft of your essay. Remember to support all of your points with examples, facts, references to reading, etc.

Review and revise: Exchange essays with a classmate. Using the Holistic scoring guide on page 252, score your partner's essay (while he or she scores yours). If necessary, rewrite your essay to correct the problems indicated by the essay's score.

Improving Paragraphs

Read the following passage and then answer the multiple-choice questions that follow. The questions will require you to make decisions regarding the revision of the reading selection.

(1) Any day of the week, between 10:00 AM and eleven PM, drop by a major bookstore. (2) You will see why movies and television will never replace written literature: people simply love to hold a book. (3) They find excitement, comfort, adventure, and familiarity in both handling and reading books.

(4) Holding a book transports the reader to earlier times, even to the happiness of childhood, when we snuggled up for that last story before bedtime. (5) Bedtime stories taught us to associate the closeness of a parent, the safety of home, and the joy of a story; on the contrary, some remnant of this satisfaction carries over to our more mature encounters with books. (6) The physicality of those experiences is somehow enclosed within the covers of every new book we touch.

(7) Even the smell of a book is captivating. (8) The smell of a book of photographs takes us back to the time when we pored over pictures, trying to imagine the motion of Willie Mays climbing the wall for "The Catch," or searching the faces of soldiers to understand their feelings before they landed on the beaches of Normandy. (9) The pulp-smell of an old book can bring back the memories of discovering classics like *Jane Eyre, Wuthering Heights,* or *Pride and Prejudice,* books that carried us through long summers at a grandmother's house. (10) The same smell, though, reminds us of finally being forced to open up a copy of *David Copperfield* to fulfill a summer reading list, so it is not always a good experience. (11) Connecting books with smell is only natural; smell is, after all, the most memorable sense for humans.

(12) While very few people read reference books for fun, many researchers prefer books to online databases, which are usually inundated with pop-up windows and advertisements. (13) With books, readers can use paper bookmarks to easily compare several sources simultaneously. (14) Advanced publishing technology have shortened the time required to print new books, giving many reference books faster production cycles and making them easier to update frequently. (15) While some material may be more current on the Internet, the intricacies of computer-based research can be daunting for many researchers; the ability to make textual comparisons is circumscribed, and the problems of documenting source material are multiplied.

(16) The peculiar relationship between writer and reader is best felt through the medium of a book. (17) A book, sometimes even a particular edition, casts a spell on the reader by which he or she can explore the mind or heart of the author. (18) The relationship is apparent in the way that a child reads and deeply experiences a picture book, returning to it repeatedly and treasuring the experience for years. (19) This experience melds the intellectual with the tactile, the cognitive with the emotional, and the personal with the universal; it is unique to the reader, the author, and the book that ties them together.

1. Which choice best corrects an error in sentence 1?
   A. remove the comma after *week*
   B. remove the comma after *eleven PM*
   C. replace *10:00 AM and eleven PM* with *ten AM and 11:00 PM*
   D. replace *drop* with *stop*
   E. replace *eleven PM* with *11:00 PM*

2. In sentence 5, *on the contrary* should be replaced with
   A. if only
   B. indeed
   C. even so
   D. after all
   E. in simpler terms

3. Which sentence of paragraph 3 is antithetical to the intent of the passage?
   A. sentence 7
   B. sentence 8
   C. sentence 9
   D. sentence 10
   E. sentence 11

4. Which choice best describes a grammatical error in sentence 14?
   A. subject-verb agreement error
   B. run-on sentence
   C. improper capitalization
   D. comma splice
   E. sentence fragment

5. If one paragraph had to be deleted from this passage, which one could be deleted without affecting the author's main idea?
   A. paragraph 1
   B. paragraph 2
   C. paragraph 3
   D. paragraph 4
   E. paragraph 5

Lesson Twenty

1. **echelon** (esh´ ə lon) *n.* a level of authority or responsibility; a rank
   Workers in the management *echelon* of the company were happy, but the laborers were about to go on strike.
   syn: level

2. **waive** (wāv) *v.* to relinquish something voluntarily; to refrain from enforcing
   Before testing the new medicine, he *waived* his right to sue the drug company.
   syn: forfeit; cede; defer   *ant: demand; enforce; impose*

3. **serendipity** (ser ən dip´ i tē) *n.* a knack or faculty of making fortunate discoveries by accident
   The discovery of penicillin is attributed to *serendipity* because the mold's properties were first observed when it was inadvertently allowed to contaminate a different experiment.
   syn: luck

4. **nondescript** (non di skript´) *adj.* lacking individual or distinct characteristics
   The private investigator drove a *nondescript* car so she could keep a low profile.
   syn: uninteresting; common; ordinary   *ant: unusual; unique; extraordinary*

5. **punitive** (pyōō´ ni tiv) *adj.* punishing; pertaining to punishment
   The government enacted *punitive* trade restrictions on any nation that refused to comply with new environmental laws.
   syn: disciplinary; corrective; retaliatory

6. **discerning** (di sûr´ ning) *adj.* having keen perception
   The *discerning* hunter spotted a deer hundreds of yards away.
   syn: perceptive; sharp; astute

7. **idyllic** (īdil´ ik) *adj.* simple and carefree; delightfully serene
   A hurricane ruined our plans for an *idyllic* vacation at the beach house.
   syn: charming; picturesque; pleasant   *ant: unpleasant; oppressive; dire*

8. **acme** (ak´ mē) *n.* the highest point
   Winning the championship game was the *acme* of the season.
   syn: pinnacle; climax; peak   *ant: nadir*

9. **soluble** (sol´ yə bəl) *adj.* easily dissolved
The packets contain *soluble* powder for making iced tea.
ant: insoluble

10. **malinger** (mə ling´ gər) *v.* to feign illness to avoid work
Scott *malingered* so often that no one believed him when he was actually ill.
syn: shirk

11. **cerebral** (ser ə´ brəl) *adj.* favoring intelligence over emotions or instinct
The dry novel had more *cerebral* appeal than displays of drama.
syn: intellectual; rational; logical   *ant: intuitive; instinctive*

12. **hypocrisy** (hi pok´ ri sē) *n.* professing beliefs, feelings, or values that one does not have or practice
In an act of complete *hypocrisy*, the actress who complains about the overuse of fossil fuels bought a second private jet.
syn: insincerity; duplicity   *ant: sincerity; earnestness*

13. **conundrum** (kə nun´ drəm) *n.* a difficult problem
The police officer faced quite a *conundrum* when he caught his own son shoplifting.
syn: quandary; predicament

14. **deleterious** (del i tēr´ ē əs) *adj.* having a harmful effect; injurious
Many people simply ignore the *deleterious* effects of prolonged exposure to the sun.
syn: destructive; pernicious; damaging   *ant: beneficial; harmless; benign*

15. **relegate** (rel´ i gāt) *v.* to place in an unfavorable place or position
The tsar *relegated* his political enemies to the freezing tundra of Siberia.
syn: demote; displace; exile

EXERCISE I—Words in Context

From the list below, supply the words needed to complete the paragraph. Some words will not be used.

soluble	echelon	punitive	waive
idyllic	discerning	deleterious	

1. The garage contained three generations of family junk, but Carla's _____ eye easily noticed the broken antique thermometer on the floor. She carefully picked it up, balancing the exposed blob of mercury on the top of the thermometer's tin backing. She knew that mercury fumes were _____ to good health, but she didn't realize that gold is _____ in liquid mercury until a drop of the substance dissolved a portion of her wedding ring. As she stared in disbelief at her ring, Carla easily thought of a few _____ chores for her son, who had knocked the old thermometer to the floor and then left to enjoy a[n] _____ summer day with his friends.

From the list below, supply the words needed to complete the paragraph. Some words will not be used.

cerebral	relegate	echelon	serendipity
conundrum	malinger	nondescript	

2. Newman faced a _____ at work. He had to inform the higher _____ that what began as a[n] _____ typographical error in the company's software was now threatening the stability of the entire company network; however, Newman himself was responsible for the error. He assumed that management, upon hearing the bad news, would _____ him to a demeaning job in the mail room, but to his surprise, the bosses were overjoyed that Newman had spotted the error before any major damage had been done. Newman decided not to inform them that his catch was a result of pure _____; he had found the error only because he had accidentally selected the wrong software to edit that day.

From the list below, supply the words needed to complete the paragraph. Some words will not be used.

acme	malinger	cerebral	punitive
hypocrisy	nondescript	waive	

3.   Tension at the civic association reached its _____ when Fred accused the governing council of _____. Fred claimed that the charter members _____ their own membership fees, and most of them _____ when the organization conducted activities that did not directly benefit its leaders. Council members accused Fred of making false accusations, but he said that it didn't take a[n] _____ giant to figure out that the leaders had been engaging in crooked practices.

EXERCISE II—Sentence Completion

Complete the sentence in a way that shows you understand the meaning of the italicized vocabulary word.

1. The college might *waive* the requirement to take English 101 if you can prove that...

2. A *discerning* collector will be able to...

3. Sam, orphaned since the age of four, did not have the *idyllic*...

4. The politician's *hypocrisy* became apparent when she made a speech about protecting wildlife and then approved...

5. When the upper *echelon* of the company noticed Sandra's talent for eliminating unnecessary expenses, the board of directors decided to...

6. In addition to fines and court costs, the company had to pay *punitive* damages meant to...

7. Discovering the ancient treasure was the *acme* of...

8. That car's leaking radiator is *deleterious* to...

9. After several disciplinary problems, Adam's parents decided to *relegate* their son to...

10. After an hour of reading the *cerebral* articles in the textbook, Matt just wanted to...

11. Sugar cubes are *soluble* in water, so if they get damp, they might...

12. The mechanic had to rely upon his own *serendipity* to fix the boat motor because...

13. Paul always *malingers* on days when...

14. The *nondescript* van outside looked like a common delivery truck, but it was actually...

15. The adventurers found themselves in a *conundrum* when they encountered...

EXERCISE III—Roots, Prefixes, and Suffixes

Study the entries and answer the questions that follow.

The root *pol* means "city."
The root *civ* means "citizen."
The root *urb* means "city."
The prefix *mega* means "large."
The prefix *sub* means "under."

1. *Using literal translations as guidance, define the following words without using a dictionary.*

   A. suburban   D. megalopolis
   B. civic   E. civilian
   C. urbanize   F. civil

2. The word *urbane* means "smooth," "polished," or "charming." Explain the possible reason for this word containing the root *urb*.

3. During a city council election, _____ might go door-to-door and ask you for your vote; however, if they refuse to leave your property, you might need to call the _____.

4. The prefix *metro* means "mother." What, literally, is a *metropolis*?

5. List as many words as you can think of that contain the prefix *sub*.

EXERCISE IV—Inference

Complete the sentences by inferring information about the italicized word from its context.

1. If Bill *waives* his rights of ownership in order to have his manuscript published, then he will not...

2. A person who prefers *cerebral* books about philosophy or science would probably not...

3. A scientist might attribute his or her success to *serendipity* if he or she did not intentionally...

EXERCISE V—Critical Reading

Below is a pair of reading passages followed by several multiple-choice questions similar to the ones you will encounter on the SAT. Carefully read both passages and choose the best answer to each of the questions.

Victor Hugo, famous for works such as Les Miserables, *which depicts life during the French Revolution, had a son, Charles, who was accused of criticizing the public execution of a man. In passage 1, delivered in 1851, Hugo entreats the court to grant mercy in sentencing his son.*

Socrates, one of the greatest philosophers in world history, was executed in 399 B.C. Passage 2 recounts parts of Socrates' last speech before the judges of the Greek court condemned him to death.

Passage 1

GENTLEMEN OF THE JURY:—If there is a culprit here, it is not my son—it is myself—it is I!—I, who for these last twenty-five years have opposed capital Punishment—have contended for the inviolability of human life—have committed this crime, for which my son is now arraigned. Here I denounce myself, Mr.
5   Advocate General! I have committed it under all aggravated circumstance—deliberately, repeatedly, tenaciously. Yes, this old and absurd *lex talionis*—this law of blood for blood—I have combated all my life—all my life, gentlemen of the jury! And, while I have breath, I will continue to combat it, by all my efforts as a writer, by all my words and all my votes as a legislator! I declare it before the crucifix;
10 before that victim of the penalty of death, who sees and hears us; before that gibbet, to which, two thousand years ago, for the eternal instruction of the generations, the human law nailed the Divine!

In all that my son has written on the subject of capital punishment—and for writing and publishing which he is now before you on trial—in all that he has writ-
15 ten, he has merely proclaimed the sentiments with which, from his infancy, I have inspired him. Gentlemen jurors, the right to criticize a law, and to criticize it severely—especially a penal law—is placed beside the duty of amelioration, like a torch beside the work under the artisan's hand. This right of the journalist is as sacred, as necessary, as imprescriptible, as the right of the legislator.
20 What are the circumstances? A man, a convict, a sentenced wretch, is dragged, on a certain morning, to one of our public squares. There he finds the scaffold! He shudders, he struggles, he refuses to die. He is young yet—only twenty-nine. Ah! I know what you will say—"He is a murderer!" But hear me. Two officers seize him. His hands, his feet, are tied. He throws off the two officers. A frightful struggle
25 ensues. His feet, bound as they are, become entangled in the ladder. He uses the scaffold against the scaffold! The struggle is prolonged. Horror seizes on the crowd. The officers—sweat and shame on their brows—pale, panting, terrified, despair-ing—despairing with I know not what horrible despair—shrinking under that pub-lic reprobation which ought to have visited the penalty, and spared the passive
30 instrument, the executioner—the officers strive savagely. The victim clings to the scaffold and shrieks for pardon. His clothes are torn—his shoulders bloody—still he resists.

At length, after three-quarters of an hour of this monstrous effort, of this specta-cle without a name, of this agony—agony for all, be it understood—agony for the
35 assembled spectators as well as for the condemned man—after this age of anguish, gentlemen of the jury, they take back the poor wretch to his prison. The people breathe again. The people, naturally merciful, hope that the man will be spared. But no—the guillotine, though vanquished, remains standing. There it frowns all day in the midst of a sickened population. And at night, the officers, reinforced, drag
40 forth the wretch again, so bound that he is but an inert weight—they drag him forth, haggard, bloody, weeping, pleading, howling for life—calling upon God, call-ing upon his father and mother—for like a very child had this man become in the prospect of death—they drag him forth to execution. He is hoisted on to the scaf-fold, and his head falls! And then through every conscience runs a shudder.

Passage 2

FOR the sake of no long space of time, O Athenians, you will incur the character and reproach at the hands of those who wish to defame the city, of having put that wise man, Socrates, to death. For those who wish to defame you will assert that I am wise, tho I am not. If, then, you had waited for a short time, this would have
5   happened of its own accord; for observe my age, that it is far advanced in life, and near death. But I say this not to you all, but to those only who have condemned me to die. And I say this too to the same persons. Perhaps you think, O Athenians, that I have been convicted through the want of arguments, by which I might have persuaded you, had I thought it right to do and say anything so that I might escape
10 punishment. Far otherwise: I have been convicted through want indeed, yet not of arguments, but of audacity and impudence, and of the inclination to say such things to you as would have been most agreeable for you to hear, had I lamented and bewailed and done and said many other things unworthy of me, as I affirm, but such as you are accustomed to hear from others.

15 But neither did I then think that I ought, for the sake of avoiding danger, to do anything unworthy of a freeman, nor do I now repent of having so defended myself; but I should much rather choose to die having so defended myself than to live in that way. For neither in a trial nor in battle is it right that I or any one else should employ every possible means whereby he may avoid death; for in battle it is fre-
20 quently evident that a man might escape death by laying down his arms and throwing himself on the mercy of his pursuers. And there are many other devices in every danger, by which to avoid death, if a man dares to do and say everything.

But this is not difficult, O Athenians, to escape death, but it is much more difficult to avoid depravity, for it runs swifter than death. And now I, being slow and
25 aged, am overtaken by the slower of the two; but my accusers, being strong and active, have been overtaken by the swifter, wickedness. And now I depart, condemned by you to death; but they condemned by truth, as guilty of iniquity and injustice: and I abide my sentence and so do they. These things, perhaps, ought so to be, and I think that they are for the best.

30 In the next place, I desire to predict to you who have condemned me, what will be your fate: for I am now in that condition in which men most frequently prophesy, namely, when they are about to die. I say then to you, O Athenians, who have condemned me to death, that immediately after my death a punishment will overtake you, far more severe, by Jupiter, than that which you have inflicted on me. For
35 you have done this thinking you should be freed from the necessity of giving an account of your life. The very contrary however, as I affirm, will happen to you. Your accusers will be more numerous, whom I have now restrained, though you did not perceive it; and they will be more severe, inasmuch as they are younger and you will be more indignant. For, if you think that by putting men to death you will
40 restrain any one from upbraiding you because you do not live well, you are much mistaken; for this method of escape is neither possible nor honorable, but that other is most honorable and most easy, not to put a check upon others, but for a man to take heed to himself, how he may be most perfect. Having predicted thus much to those of you who have condemned me, I take my leave of you.

45 But with you who have voted for my acquittal, I would gladly hold converse on what has now taken place, while the magistrates are busy and I am not yet carried

to the place where I must die. Stay with me then, so long, O Athenians, for nothing hinders our conversing with each other, whilst we are permitted to do so; for I wish to make known to you, as being my friends, the meaning of that which has
50   just now befallen me. To me then, O my judges—and in calling you judges I call you rightly—a strange thing has happened. For the wonted prophetic voice of my guardian deity, on every former occasion, even in the most trifling affairs, opposed me, if I was about to do anything wrong; but now, that has befallen me which ye yourselves behold, and which any one would think and which is supposed to be
55   the extremity of evil, yet neither when I departed from home in the morning did the warning of the god oppose me, nor when I came up here to the place of trial, nor in my address when I was about to say anything; yet on other occasions it has frequently restrained me in the midst of speaking. But now it has never throughout this proceeding opposed me, either in what I did or said. What then do I suppose
60   to be the cause of this? I will tell you: what has befallen me appears to be a blessing; and it is impossible that we think rightly who suppose that death is an evil. A great proof of this to me is the fact that it is impossible but that the accustomed signal should have opposed me, unless I had been about to meet with some good.

[. . .]

You, therefore, O my judges, ought to entertain good hopes with respect to death,
65   and to meditate on this one truth, that to a good man nothing is evil, neither while living nor when dead, nor are his concerns neglected by the gods. And what has befallen me is not the effect of chance; but this is clear to me, that now to die, and be freed from my cares, is better for me. On this account the warning in no way turned me aside; and I bear no resentment toward those who condemned me, or
70   against my accusers, although they did not condemn and accuse me with this intention, but thinking to injure me: in this they deserve to be blamed.

Thus much, however, I beg of them. Punish my sons, when they grow up, O judges, paining them as I have pained you, if they appear to you to care for riches or anything else before virtue, and if they think themselves to be something when
75   they are nothing, reproach them as I have done you, for not attending to what they ought, and for conceiving themselves to be something when they are worth nothing. If ye do this, both I and my sons shall have met with just treatment at your hands.

But it is now time to depart,—for me to die, for you to live. But which of us is
80   going to a better state is unknown to every one but God.

1. Which choice best paraphrases the following quotation from passage 1?

   > Gentlemen jurors, the right to criticize a law, and to criticize it severely—especially a penal law—is placed beside the duty of amelioration, like a torch beside the work under the artisan's hand.

   A. Thorough criticism is essential to the improvement of law.
   B. Legislation will always be criticized.
   C. Gentlemen work with criticism as an artist works with clay.
   D. The penal law cannot be harmed by constructive criticism.
   E. Criticism is even more important than duty to uphold the law.

2. Paragraph 3 of first passage has the purpose of
   A. explaining that the criminal escaped justice.
   B. describing the son's horrible demise.
   C. describing the scene that the son criticized.
   D. explaining that the government should charge admission.
   E. discounting the credibility of the court officials.

3. The author personifies the guillotine in the final paragraph of passage 1 by suggesting
   A. that the condemned man has escaped the guillotine before.
   B. that the public claims to see ghosts around the device.
   C. that the public disapproves of a killing device in the square.
   D. that the guillotine is sympathetic to the criminal's misfortune.
   E. that the guillotine is angry for having to wait for the execution.

4. As used in line 8 of passage 2, *want* most nearly means
   A. desire.
   B. lack.
   C. famine.
   D. choice.
   E. like.

5. According to paragraph 3 of the second passage, the accusers are guilty of
   A. theft.
   B. revenge.
   C. mercy.
   D. corruption
   E. rejection.

6. Socrates demands that his sons be punished if they
   A. become government officials.
   B. take too much interest in wealth.
   C. refuse to attend their father's burial.
   D. do not follow the teachings of Plato.
   E. speak out against the government.

7. In both passages, the subject involves people on trial for
   A. extorting government funds.
   B. harboring fugitives.
   C. leading revolutions.
   D. communicating with the enemy.
   E. subversive speech.

8. The two authors might *not* agree with each other about which one of the following statements?
   A. Capital punishment can have negative effects upon the public.
   B. Citizens must be watchful of the government.
   C. One should never speak out against government policies.
   D. One should attempt every possible option to escape death.
   E. There are problems with capital punishment.

9. The narrators of each passage are different in that
   A. one is a philosopher, and the other is a soldier.
   B. one defends capital punishment, and the other condemns it.
   C. one is defending himself, while the other is defending his son.
   D. one has two sons being tried, and the other has only one.
   E. one appears to be relieved, while the other is horrified.

10. Which choice best contrasts the basis of each author's argument?
    A. Hugo demands that his son be held culpable, while Socrates attempts to atone for his crimes.
    B. Passage 1 is persuasive, while passage 2 is informative.
    C. Passage 1 emphasizes rhetoric, and passage 2 contains abundant physical descriptions.
    D. Passage 1 is written in third-person point of view, and passage 2 is pastoral.
    E. Hugo appeals to the compassion of the court, but Socrates warns of consequences that will follow his death.

Lesson Twenty-One

1. **propinquity** (prə ping´ kwi tē) *n.* nearness; proximity
His *propinquity* to both murders made Tom a suspect.
syn: closeness; immediacy; adjacency   *ant: distance; remoteness*

2. **abrogate** (ab´ rə gāt) *v.* to abolish, especially by authority; to revoke
formally
The town council voted to *abrogate* the unpopular law.
syn: annul; invalidate; repeal   *ant: establish; ratify; support*

3. **supine** (sōō pīn´) *adj.* lying on one's back; lying face-up
The hero lay helplessly *supine* in the villain's library after falling victim to
the knockout gas.
ant: prone

4. **prosaic** (prō zā´ ik) *adj.* straightforward and unimaginative;
uninteresting
After missing my curfew, I had to sit through yet another boring, *prosaic*
speech on family rules.
syn: banal; humdrum; monotonous   *ant: fascinating; inspiring*

5. **parity** (par´ i tē) *n.* equality
North and South Korea have no economic *parity*.
syn: balance; equivalence; proportion   *ant: disparity; imbalance*

6. **extrinsic** (ik strin´ sik) *adj.* not essential; extraneous
To make the aircraft lighter, the crew removed *extrinsic* parts not required
for flight.
syn: unnecessary; adventitious   *ant: necessary; crucial;*
required; intrinsic

7. **outré** (ōō trā´) *adj.* extremely unconventional; bizarre
Malcolm had an *outré* personality that made him well known for his odd
behavior.
syn: eccentric; freaky; outlandish   *ant: conforming; ordinary*

8. **analects** (an´ ə lekts) *n.* selections from a literary work
The Eastern philosophy class discussed the *analects* of Confucius.

9. **surreptitious** (sûr əp tish´ əs) *adj.* accomplished through stealth and secrecy
Smiling and nodding, the man cast a *surreptitious* glance at his watch while listening to his chatty neighbor.
syn: furtive; sneaky; clandestine   *ant: open; candid*

10. **anomie** (an´ ə mē) *n.* societal or personal instability caused by a lack or erosion of values, standards, or ideals
The Roman Empire ruled the world until widespread *anomie*, fueled by corruption, caused its decline.

11. **magniloquent** (mag nil´ ə kwənt) *adj.* lofty in expression; pompous
In a *magniloquent* voice, the herald announced the arrival of the royal family.
syn: grandiloquent; grandiose; ostentatious   *ant: humble; subtle; reserved*

12. **factotum** (fak tō´ təm) *n.* an employee with a variety of jobs or responsibilities
As a *factotum* for the family business, Craig did the jobs of three employees.
syn: workhorse; operator   *ant: principal*

13. **cognizant** (käg´ nə zənt) *adj.* fully informed; having knowledge of
Ben nodded his head, pretending to be *cognizant* of what the teacher was talking about.
syn: aware; perceptive; sentient   *ant: ignorant; unaware; oblivious*

14. **febrile** (fe´ brīl) *adj.* pertaining to fever; feverish
The *febrile* child was sent home from school to recover.

15. **apostasy** (ə päs´ tə sē) *n.* abandonment of one's principles, faith, or religious beliefs
Government officials doubted the genuineness of the former spy's sudden *apostasy*.
syn: defection; disavowal; renunciation   *ant: commitment; dedication; loyalty*

EXERCISE I—Words in Context

From the list below, supply the words needed to complete the paragraph. Some words will not be used.

outré	prosaic	propinquity	analects
surreptitious	cognizant	supine	

1.   None of the guards noticed Alistair's _____ entry into the secret compound. The investigative reporter, known for his _____ strategies in obtaining information, had ridden through the gates beneath a supply truck, and now he lay _____ on the ground beneath the vehicle, searching for potential hiding places. He grimaced when he became _____ of the anthill directly beneath his shoulders, but he made no sound because of the _____ of the guards in front of the truck.

From the list below, supply the words needed to complete the paragraph. Some words will not be used.

factotum	cognizant	prosaic	extrinsic
magniloquent	parity	abrogate	

2.   When the government _____ the use of clandestine agents as assassins and saboteurs, the CIA was forced to find new methods of dealing with foreign threats and interests. Mr. Bell was one of those methods. According to his personnel file, Mr. Bell was simply a "program manager" at the Pentagon; however, despite the bland job title, he was one of many _____ whose duty was to resolve those international problems that simple, public diplomacy cannot solve.

    Mr. Bell, whose real name is known only to his employer, gained most of his experience during the Cold War, when his primary mission was to ensure that the United States maintained defensive _____ with the Soviet Union. The work did include rare moments of extreme stress, but, to the disappointment of spy-thriller movie fans, the job most often involved hours of reading _____ logistics documents, most of which contained only _____ information that had little bearing on national security.

From the list below, supply the words needed to complete the paragraph. Some words will not be used.

supine	analects	febrile	magniloquent
parity	anomie	apostasy	

3.   Pete regretted his _____ from the simple life and desires he had before the massive failure of his dot-com endeavor. Like many other young entrepreneurs, Pete had allowed _____ to overtake him as he fixated on his monthly profit margins and failed to invest in advertising or customer service. Now he was bankrupt, and he watched as movers carried his _____ dining room furniture out the door of his house to the waiting moving truck and eventually to a public auction.

At moments, Pete's anger over his own poor judgment made him red-faced and _____, but he quickly recovered when he thought of a new marketing idea: he would create a best-selling novel that featured the personal accounts of the hundreds of failed dot-com business owners. The _____ of the failed owners would be excellent guidance for inexperienced entrepreneurs, like Pete, and also for investors.

EXERCISE II—Sentence Completion

Complete the sentence in a way that shows you understand the meaning of the italicized vocabulary word.

1. Madeline grew weary of being a *factotum* with the responsibilities of...

2. There is little *parity* in the quality of the hotel rooms; one room might look clean and new, while another room...

3. Detective Stone of the white-collar crimes division never understood the *apostasy* that caused successful people with wonderful families to...

4. Young Ralphie looked *febrile* this morning, so his mother...

5. As soon as the iron filings are in *propinquity* to the magnet, they...

6. Bored after sitting in the waiting room for an hour, Lenny picked up a *prosaic* pamphlet about...

7. Fiction and movies often depict the American Wild West as a place of *anomie*, where bounty hunters had routine gunfights with outlaws, and inhabitants could not rely on laws to...

8. The camper was not *cognizant* of the rattlesnake in her tent until...

9. The man's *outré* sales pitch involved the use of...

10. The English teacher said that the *extrinsic* information in the essay merely...

11. It took the spy five years to earn the *surreptitious* cover of...

12. When a passing policeman saw customers in the bank lying *supine*, he knew that...

13. Derek's parents *abrogated* his access to the computer after...

14. The students discussed *analects* from *The Adventures of Huckleberry Finn* while studying...

15. The narrator of the automobile commercial explained in a *magniloquent* voice why the featured car was...

EXERCISE III—Roots, Prefixes, and Suffixes

Study the entries and answer the questions that follow.

The roots *cur* and *curs* mean "to run."
The root *ambul* means "to walk."
The prefix *ob* means "in the way of" or "against."
The prefix *per* means "through."

1. *Using literal translations as guidance, define the following words without using a dictionary.*

    A. current   D. amble
    B. ambulatory   E. occur
    C. cursive   F. perambulate

2. In the sentence, "John made a *cursory* inspection of his luggage," does the word *cursory* mean "fast," or "slow"?
    Explain why the blinking prompt on the display of a computer screen is called a *cursor*.

3. The root *somn* means sleep. If a person *somnambulates*, what is he or she doing?

4. A *current* is a flowing of something, or a passing from one person to another, so it is appropriate that coin or paper money, which circulates among people, is called _____.

5. List as many words as you can think of that contain the prefix *ob*.

EXERCISE IV—Inference

Complete the sentences by inferring information about the italicized word from its context.

1. If a religious sect experiences widespread *apostasy*, then members are probably...

2. In a household with many children, *parity* of parental attention might be difficult to maintain because...

3. The government might be forced to *abrogate* an unpopular law if...

EXERCISE V—Writing

Here is a writing prompt similar to the one you will find on the writing portion of the SAT.

Plan and write an essay based on the following statement:

> As in political so in literary action a man wins friends
> for himself mostly by the passion of his prejudices and
> the consistent narrowness of his outlook.
> – Joseph Conrad (1857–1924)

Assignment: Think of the things that you look for in a friend and determine whether you agree or disagree with Joseph Conrad's statement. In an essay, defend or refute Conrad's suggestion that a narrow outlook might have value in literature. Support your essay with evidence from literature, history, or experience or observation.

Thesis: Write a one-sentence response to the above assignment. Make certain this sentence offers a clear statement of your position.

Example: If not for the unique, narrow outlook of writers, the world would be absent of any great literature, for it is that unique perspective that attracts and fixes the attention of both readers and critics alike.

Organizational Plan: If your thesis is the point on which you want to end, where does your essay need to begin? List the points of development that are inevitable in leading your reader from your beginning point to your end point. This list is your outline.

Draft: Use your thesis as both your beginning and your end. Following your outline, write a good first draft of your essay. Remember to support all of your points with examples, facts, references to reading, etc.

Review and revise: Exchange essays with a classmate. Using the Holistic scoring guide on page 252, score your partner's essay (while he or she scores yours). If necessary, rewrite your essay to correct the problems indicated by the essay's score.

Identifying Sentence Errors

Identify the grammatical error in each of the following sentences. If the sentence contains no error, select answer E.

1. <u>None of the students</u> in gym class <u>were dressed</u> for calisthenics
       (A)   (B)
   <u>because the teacher</u> made them <u>exercise too many</u> times.   <u>No error</u>
     (C)   (D)   (E)

2. <u>We could</u> not account <u>for our loss,</u> <u>not even after we went</u> over our bank
      (A)   (B)   (C)
   <u>statement</u>.   <u>No error</u>
      (D)   (E)

3. <u>We need</u> to <u>make a decision</u> about <u>which of the three</u> plans
      (A)   (B)   (C)
   <u>is more advantageous.</u>   <u>No error</u>
        (D)   (E)

4. If you have any <u>questions, please</u> contact <u>myself</u> or <u>any other teacher</u> on
                        (A)   (B)   (C)
   duty <u>who can help you</u> with the test.   <u>No error</u>
             (D)   (E)

5. <u>You will have</u> to <u>speak quick</u> to have <u>your message go into</u> the
        (A)   (B)   (C)
   <u>company's voice mail</u>.   <u>No error</u>
        (D)   (E)

Improving Sentences

The underlined portion of each sentence below contains some flaw. Select the answer that best corrects the flaw.

6. If the boys had been in the shed, <u>they would not hear the loud explosion, but since they were in the yard, they did notice the noise.</u>
   A. they could not hear the loud explosion, but since they were in the yard, they didn't notice the noise.
   B. they would not have heard the loud explosion, but since they were in the yard, they did notice the noise.
   C. they would not hear the loud explosion; since they were in the yard, they noticed the noise.
   D. they were unable to have heard the loud explosion, but since they were in the yard, they did notice the noise.
   E. they would not hear the loud explosion, since they were in the yard; they noticed the noise.

7. Many people believe <u>that the reason dinosaurs became extinct is because</u> the Earth's climate changed.
   A. that the reason the dinosaurs went extinct is because
   B. the reason dinosaurs became extinct is
   C. that dinosaurs became extinct when
   D. that dinosaurs became extinct because
   E. that the reason behind dinosaurs being extinct is because

8. <u>Between the three candidates, no one achieved a majority of the votes,</u> and there was a run-off election.
   A. Between the three candidates, no one achieved a large-enough majority of the votes,
   B. Among the three candidates, no one achieved a majority of the votes,
   C. Not one of the three candidates achieved a majority of the votes cast,
   D. Among the three candidates, no one achieved a plurality of the votes,
   E. Between the three candidates, no one achieved the plurality the votes,

9. Either the twins, the triplets, or the baby <u>have won the prize for being the most beautiful child in the contest.</u>
    A. has won the prize of the most beautiful child in the contest.
    B. has won the prize for being the most beautiful child in the contest.
    C. has won the prize for the most beautiful child in the contest.
    D. has won the contest by winning the most beautiful child competition.
    E. wins the prize for being the most beautiful child in the contest.

10. <u>So cold that his fingers would not move, a fire could not be built because the match was not able to be struck by the prospector.</u>
    A. The cold fingers of the prospector were unable to build a fire by striking the matches.
    B. The matches were cold, the prospector could not move his fingers, and a fire could not be built.
    C. So cold were the prospector's fingers that he could not build a fire by striking a match
    D. The prospector's cold fingers were unable to strike the match, thus leaving him unable to build the fire.
    E. The prospector's fingers were so cold that he could not strike a match to build a fire.

REVIEW

Lessons 15 – 21

EXERCISE I – Sentence Completion

Choose the best pair of words to complete the sentence. Most choices will fit grammatically and will even make sense logically, but you must choose the pair that best fits the idea of the sentence.

Note that these words are not taken directly from lessons in this book. This exercise is intended to replicate the sentence completion portion of the SAT.

1. The _____ for the word was unknown to Jonathon, so he used a[n] _____ to find a few of them.
   A. meaning, encyclopedia
   B. pronunciation, almanac
   C. antonym, thesaurus
   D. definition, friend
   E. synonym, guess

2. When Shakespeare wrote his plays, few people in England had ever been in a[n] _____, let alone seen a live _____.
   A. play, act
   B. theater, performance
   C. audience, concert
   D. situation, dramatization
   E. crowd, play

3. Given enough food and sunlight, most plants will grow _____, but my vegetables cannot seem to _____, no matter what I do.
   A. quickly, stay
   B. amazingly, live
   C. skyward, survive
   D. tall, prosper
   E. vigorously, thrive

4. _____, the little girl picked up the bird that had fallen from its nest and replaced it before its parents _____.
   A. Gently, returned
   B. Strenuously, arrived
   C. Rapidly, knew
   D. Quietly, observed
   E. Helen, chirped

5. The doctor was _____ to inform the boy's parents that their child had a rare and _____ fatal disease.
   A. anxious, sometimes
   B. hesitant, ultimately
   C. proposing, always
   D. preparing, extremely
   E. reluctant, completely

6. The _____ _____ nearly an entire city block before anyone arrived on the scene to help.
   A. crime, destroyed
   B. weather, covered
   C. fight, blanketed
   D. explosion, corrupted
   E. blaze, consumed

7. After they arrived with their parents, the children immediately _____ to go see the rare, _____ species of monkey that the zoo had displayed for only a few months.
   A. cried, wild
   B. clamored, endangered
   C. begged, controversial
   D. demanded, phenomenal
   E. wanted, extinct

8. Dan began taking the math test with _____ because the previous night, he had _____ studying for it.
   A. fear, forgotten
   B. hatred, demeaned
   C. eagerness, tried
   D. trepidation, enjoyed
   E. anxiety, avoided

EXERCISE II – Crossword Puzzle

Use the clues to complete the crossword puzzle. The answers consist of vocabulary words from lessons 15 through 21.

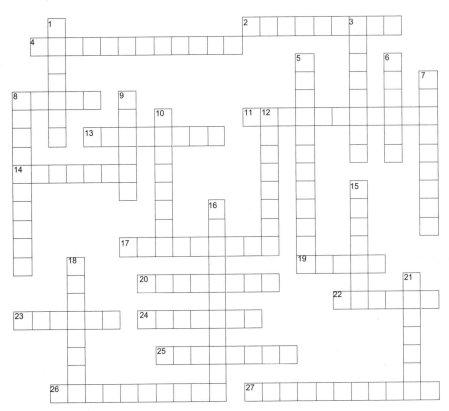

Across
2. moral corruption
4. compensation; payment
8. overused; hackneyed
11. name or title
13. employee with various duties
14. a level of authority; rank
17. to eradicate
19. descendant; heir
20. swiftness in action; speed

22. easily excused
23. equality
24. to suppress
25. formal praise
26. promising; auspicious
27. nearness

Down
1. to repeal
3. undeveloped
5. contemptuous; arrogant
6. lying face-up

7. difficult problem
8. digressing from the main point
9. known by only a few
10. very moving; touching
12. punishing
15. offensively flattering
16. unnecessary; excessive
18. to feign illness to avoid work
21. coming into existence

Scoring Guide for the SAT Writing Test

ORGANIZATION

6 = Clearly Competent

The paper is clearly **organized** around the central point or main idea.
The work is **free of surface errors** (grammar, spelling, punctuation, etc.).

5 = Reasonably Competent

The **organizational plan** of the paper is **clear, but not fully implemented.**
Minor surface errors are present, but they **do not interfere** with the reader's understanding of the work.

4 = Adequately Competent

The **organizational plan** of the paper is **apparent, but not consistently implemented.**
Surface errors are present, but they **do not severely interfere** with the reader's understanding.

3 = Nearly Competent

There is evidence of an **organizational plan.**
Surface errors are **apparent** and **begin to interfere** with the reader's understanding of the work.

2 = Marginally Incompetent

The **organizational plan** of the writing is obscured by **too few** details and/or **irrelevant** details.
Surface errors are **frequent and severe enough** to **interfere** with the reader's understanding of the work.

1 = Incompetent

There is **no clear organizational plan** and/or **insufficient material.**
Surface errors are **frequent** and **extreme,** and **severely interfere** with the reader's understanding of the work.

Scoring Guide for the SAT Writing Test

DEVELOPMENT

6 = Clearly Competent
There is **sufficient** material (details, examples, anecdotes, supporting facts, etc.) to allow the reader to feel he/she has read a full and complete discussion without notable gaps, unanswered questions, or unexplored territory in the topic. Every word, phrase, clause, and sentence is **relevant**, contributing effectively to the thesis.
The work is **free of surface errors** (grammar, spelling, punctuation, etc.).

5 = Reasonably Competent
There is **nearly sufficient** material for a full and complete discussion, but the reader is left with **a few unanswered questions**. There is no superfluous or **irrelevant** material.
Minor surface errors are present, but they **do not interfere** with the reader's understanding of the work.

4 = Adequately Competent
There is **nearly sufficient** material for a full and complete discussion, but the reader is left with **a few unanswered questions**. Irrelevant material is present.
Surface errors are present, but they **do not severely interfere** with the reader's understanding.

3 = Nearly Competent
There is evidence of an organizational plan. There are **too few** details, examples, anecdotes, supporting facts, etc.
Surface errors are **apparent** and **begin to interfere** with the reader's understanding of the work.

2 = Marginally Incompetent
The organizational plan of the writing is obscured by **too few** details and/or **irrelevant** details.
Surface errors are **frequent and severe enough** to interfere with the reader's understanding of the work.

1 = Incompetent
The writing sample **attempts** to discuss the topic but **severely marred** because surface errors are **frequent** and **extreme**, and **severely interfere** with the reader's understanding of the work.

Scoring Guide for the SAT Writing Test

SENTENCE FORMATION AND VARIETY

6 = Clearly Competent

Sentences are **complete, grammatically correct**, and assist the reader in following the flow of the discussion. The use of a **variety** of sentence structures contributes to the effective organization of the work and the reader's understanding.

The work is **free of surface errors** (grammar, spelling, punctuation, etc.).

5 = Reasonably Competent

Sentences are **complete, generally correct**, and do not distract the reader from the flow of the discussion. There is evidence of a concerted effort to use a **variety** of structures.

Minor surface errors are present, but they **do not interfere** with the reader's understanding of the work.

4 = Adequately Competent

Sentences are **complete and generally correct**. There is evidence of a concerted effort to use a **variety** of structures.

Surface errors are present, but they **do not severely interfere** with the reader's understanding.

3 = Nearly Competent

Sentences are **generally complete and grammatically correct**, but there are errors that begin to distract the reader. Sentence structure might be accurate, but **dull or routine**.

Surface errors are **apparent** and **begin to interfere** with the reader's understanding of the work.

2 = Marginally Incompetent

Problems in **sentence structure** and **grammar** are **distracting**, and provide **little or no variety**.

Surface errors are **frequent and severe enough** to **interfere** with the reader's understanding of the work.

1 = Incompetent

Sentences are **riddled with errors**. There is **little or no variety** in sentence structure.

Surface errors are **frequent** and **extreme**, and **severely interfere** with the reader's understanding of the work.

Scoring Guide for the SAT Writing Test

WORD CHOICE

6 = Clearly Competent
> The word choice is **specific, clear, and vivid**. Powerful nouns and verbs replace weaker adjective-noun/adverb-verb phrases. Clear, specific, and accurate words replace vague, general terms.
> The work is **free of surface errors** (grammar, spelling, punctuation, etc.).

5 = Reasonably Competent
> Word choice is **clear** and **accurate**. For the most part, the writer has chosen **vivid, powerful words and phrases.**
> Sentences are **complete, generally correct**, and do not distract the reader from the flow of the discussion. There is evidence of a concerted effort to use a **variety** of structures.

4 = Adequately Competent
> Word choice is **adequate**. For the most part, the writer has chosen **vivid, powerful words and phrases.**
> **Surface errors** are present, but they **do not severely interfere** with the reader's understanding.

3 = Nearly Competent
> Word choice is **inconsistent**.
> Surface errors are **apparent** and **begin to interfere** with the reader's understanding of the work.

2 = Marginally Incompetent
> Word choice is **generally vague** with a few attempts at vividness.
> Surface errors are **frequent and severe enough** to **interfere** with the reader's understanding of the work.

1 = Incompetent
> Word choice is **lazy, inexact**, and **vague**. The writer has either too limited a vocabulary, or has not sought the best words for the topic, audience, and purpose.
> Surface errors are **frequent and extreme**, and **severely interfere** with the reader's understanding of the work.

Scoring Guide for the SAT Writing Test

HOLISTIC[1]

6 = Clearly Competent
The writing sample discusses the **topic effectively and insightfully**.

The paper is clearly **organized** around the central point or main idea. There is **sufficient** material (details, examples, anecdotes, supporting facts, etc.) to allow the reader to feel he/she has read a full and complete discussion without notable gaps, unanswered questions, or unexplored territory in the topic. Every word, phrase, clause, and sentence is **relevant**, contributing effectively to that idea.

The word choice is **specific, clear, and vivid**. Powerful nouns and verbs replace weaker adjective-noun/adverb-verb phrases. Clear, specific, and accurate words replace vague, general terms.

Sentences are **complete, grammatically correct**, and assist the reader in following the flow of the discussion. The use of a **variety** of sentence structures contributes to the effective organization of the work and the reader's understanding.

The work is **free of surface errors** (grammar, spelling, punctuation, etc.).

5 = Reasonably Competent
The writing sample discusses the **topic effectively**.

The **organizational plan** of the paper is **clear, but not fully implemented**. There is **nearly sufficient** material for a full and complete discussion, but the reader is left with **a few unanswered questions**. There is no superfluous or **irrelevant** material.

Word choice is **clear** and **accurate**. For the most part, the writer has chosen **vivid, powerful words and phrases**.

Minor surface errors are present, but they **do not interfere** with the reader's understanding of the work.

Sentences are **complete, generally correct**, and do not distract the reader from the flow of the discussion. There is evidence of a concerted effort to use a **variety** of structures.

[1] Adapted from materials appearing on www.collegeboard.com, the official website of the College Board.

4 = Adequately Competent
The writing sample **discusses the topic.**

The **organizational plan** of the paper is **apparent, but not consistently implemented.** There is **nearly sufficient** material for a full and complete discussion, but the reader is left with **a few unanswered questions.**
Word choice is **adequate.** For the most part, the writer has chosen **vivid, powerful words and phrases.**

Surface errors are present, but they **do not severely interfere** with the reader's understanding.

Sentences are **complete and generally correct.** There is evidence of a concerted effort to use a **variety** of structures.

3 = Nearly Competent
The writing sample **discusses** the **topic** but is **marred** by the following:

There is evidence of an **organizational plan.** There are **too few** details, examples, anecdotes, supporting facts, etc.

Word choice is **inconsistent.**

Sentences are **generally complete and grammatically correct**, but there are errors that begin to distract the reader. Sentence structure might be accurate, but **dull or routine.**

Surface errors are **apparent** and **begin to interfere** with the reader's understanding of the work.

2 = Marginally Incompetent
The writing sample **discusses** the **topic**, but the discussion is **marred** by the following:

The **organizational plan** of the writing is obscured by **too few** details and/or **irrelevant** details.

Word choice is **generally vague** with a few attempts at vividness.

Problems in **sentence structure** and **grammar** are **distracting**, and provide **little or no variety.**

Surface errors are **frequent and severe enough** to **interfere** with the reader's understanding of the work.

1 = Incompetent

The writing sample **attempts** to discuss the topic but is **severely marred** by the following:

There is **no clear organizational plan** and/or **insufficient material**.

Word choice is **lazy, inexact,** and **vague**. The writer has either too limited a vocabulary, or has not sought the best words for the topic, audience, and purpose.

Sentences are **riddled with errors**. There is **little or no variety** in sentence structure.

Surface errors are **frequent** and **extreme**, and **severely interfere** with the reader's understanding of the work.